Additio..... .....
for *Re-Reading Job*

2014 Best Religious Non-fiction award, Association for Mormon Letters.

"Michael Austin is entertaining. He makes relevant comments and examples from our lives that help explain the points he's trying to make about Job. . . . and, most importantly, he is emotionally engaged with the material."

— Terry L. Hutchinson, *Meridian Magazine*

"*Re-Reading Job: Understanding the Ancient World's Greatest Poem* is another fantastic title in the growing series "Contemporary Studies in Scripture" from Kofford Books. The series continues to demonstrate that scholarly approaches need not obstruct a faithful reading of scripture; scholarly approaches can actually facilitate more devotional and inspired reading."

— Neal A. Maxwell Institute for Religious Understanding, BYU

"Promises to enrich and enliven LDS discussions of scripture. Whatever its reliance on academic information and methods, it could hardly be more accessibly and clearly written. Bravo to Michael Austin for what I hope will prove to be an influential book."

— Jason Kerr, By Common Consent

"Michael Austin's *Re-Reading Job: Understanding the Ancient World's Greatest Poem* is a terrific book; smart, thoughtful, funny. I honestly didn't think a literary scholar's close reading of the (boring) Book of Job would be so compulsively readable. I didn't think it would be the kind of book I would find myself unable to put down at two o'clock in the morning. Honestly, I thought reading it would be kind of a chore; that I would trudge my way through it dutifully, seeking a nugget of enlightenment in the mucky stream of turgid prose. Instead, I got all caught up in it."

— Eric Samuelsen, Mormon Iconoclast

"This book is educational, entertaining, uncomfortable, and inspiring. A quadruple threat if ever I've seen one. Pick it up today! Highly recommended."

— David Tayman, Improvement Era

"This is a great book. Buy it. Read it. Now."

— Association for Mormon Letters

"Austin draws on scholarship that locates the origins of the Job frame tale in Persian folklore, but his reading also relies on the insights of historical biblical criticism. . . . Austin's focus on the big picture serves as a helpful introduction to deeper study of Job."

— Jason Kerr, *Studies in the Bible and Antiquity*

"It does an enormous amount of the crucial work of packaging the findings of biblical scholars for a lay audience that will allow for more serious engagement with scripture."

— Joseph Spencer, Peculiar People

Contemporary Studies in Scripture

An exciting new series from Greg Kofford Books featuring authors whose works engage in rigorous textual analyses of the Bible and other LDS scripture. Written by Latter-day Saints for a Latter-day Saint audience, these books utilize the tools of historical criticism, literature, philosophy, and the sciences to celebrate the richness and complexity found in the standard works. This series will provide readers with new and fascinating ways to read, study, and re-read these sacred texts.

Re-reading Job

Re-reading Job

Understanding the Ancient World's Greatest Poem

Michael Austin

GREG KOFFORD BOOKS
SALT LAKE CITY, 2014

2nd printing, 2016

Greg Kofford Books
P.O. Box 1362
Draper, UT 84020
www.gregkofford.com
facebook.com/gkbooks

Also available in ebook.

2018   17   16   .   .   5   4   3   2   .

Library of Congress Cataloging-in-Publication Data

Austin, Michael, 1966- author.
  Rereading Job : understanding the ancient world's greatest poem / Michael Austin.
    pages cm
  Includes bibliographical references and index.
  ISBN 978-1-58958-667-3 (pbk.) -- ISBN 978-1-58958-668-0 (hardcover)
  1. Bible. Job--Criticism, interpretation, etc. 2. Church of Jesus Christ of Latter-day Saints--Doctrines. 3. Mormon Church--Doctrines. I. Title.
  BS1415.52.A97 2014
  223'.106--dc23
                            2014017136

For Karen, my best reader

Contents

Preface

Tomorrow, if all literature was to be destroyed and it was left to me to retain one work only, I should save Job. — Victor Hugo

There is nothing written, I think, in the Bible or out of it, of equal merit. — Thomas Carlyle

The greatest poem of ancient or modern times. — Alfred Lord Tennyson

Victor Hugo, Thomas Carlyle, and Lord Tennyson were three of the greatest writers of the nineteenth century—and they were not easily impressed. They did not praise lightly, and, when they did praise, they rarely praised the same things. One thing that all three did share, though, was a deep distrust of traditional religion and traditional religious texts—except for the Book of Job. If we line up their statements about Job, they look less like the opinions of three of the greatest minds of the nineteenth century and more like the gushing reviews on the back of a recent bestseller. The Book of Job has affected people this way for nearly 2,500 years.

The greatest philosophical and literary minds of our world have long felt a powerful need to come to terms with Job: Aquinas, Maimonides, Hegel, Kant, and Kierkegaard all offered their own interpretations of Job, and John Calvin preached more sermons on Job than on any other book in the Bible. William Blake's most famous works of art are his etchings for the Book of Job. Johann Wolfgang von Goethe's masterpiece *Faust* is a retelling of the Job story. So too are Voltaire's *Candide* and Kafka's *The Trial.* Kafka's entire oeuvre, in fact, can be described as the attempt of a modern man to understand what it might have felt like to be Job.

And yet for all of this, nobody has ever quite figured out what Job means. The book famously resists any kind of narrative closure or final interpretation. The best scholars in the world still ask the very same questions about Job that the Jewish philosopher Maimonides asked 800 years ago: Does God make us suffer? Is the universe ultimately just? Is righ-teousness just a form of self-interest? Can we conceive of ultimate good-ness as something separate from ultimate power? Can human beings ever see the world from God's perspective?

These, it turns out, are some of the hardest questions that human beings have ever tried to answer. And even when the Book of Job fails to answer them (which it usually does), it has done humanity the great service of providing us with a framework for talking with each other about them. And the framework that Job created has led to art, literature, psy-chology, philosophy, and theology that have advanced works of human understanding in profound ways.

So why does the world need one more book about Job? It's not like there aren't plenty of them already. In the twenty years that I have spent trying to understand it, I have read adaptations of and books about Job from a dizzying variety of viewpoints. I know the Catholic Job (G.K. Chesterton's "Introduction to Job" and Muriel Spark's *The Comforters*), the Protestant Job (Robert Frost's *A Masque of Reason* and Archibald MacLeish's *J.B.*), and the post-Holocaust Jewish Job (Elie Wiesel's *The Trial of God* and Zvi Kolitz's "Yosl Rakover Talks to God"). I have also learned much from Job the Politician (William Safire's *The First Dissident*), Job the Education Reformer (H. G. Wells' *The Undying Fire*), and Job the Dimension-Hopping Fundamentalist Fire Walker (Robert A. Heinlein's *Job: A Comedy of Justice*). And I know more scholarly Jobs than I can fit on a reasonably sized bookshelf. But I have yet to meet a Mormon Job. Job is one of the books of the Bible that generally eludes Latter-day Saint readers. It does not fit well into the standard narratives that most Mormons bring with them to their study of the Old Testament. Latter-day Saints are not used to reading scriptures that are also poetry, nor do we usually like to focus on the parts of the scriptures that, like Job, challenge orthodox beliefs and present God as less than one hundred percent perfect. What does fit nicely into LDS interpretive traditions, though, is the short prose tale that makes up the first two chapters and the last half of the last chapter of the Book of Job. And with very few exceptions, this is what gets taught. This is a shame, as the rest of the Book of Job has some very important things to say to Latter-day Saints.

And Latter-day Saints have plenty to say about the Book of Job. Mormon theology and LDS scripture have the potential to open av-enues for interpreting Job that previous religious traditions have ignored.

Unique Mormon beliefs about things like free agency, personal revelation, the nature of God, and the role of the pre-existent Satan speak to elements of Job that have been invisible to generations of interpreters. If Latter-day Saints understood Job better, I believe that we would find it resonating with our own beliefs in remarkable ways. This is why I believe that the world has room for another book about Job.

I come to Job as a practicing member of the Church of Jesus Christ of Latter-day Saints and as a scholar of English literature specializing in the poetry and prose of the seventeenth century. In the past, I have written about such figures as Milton, Dryden, Cowley, Bunyan, and Defoe, paying close attention to the ways that they incorporated the narratives of the Old Testament into their work. I am not a scholar of Hebrew. Like most of my co-religionists, I know Job only through translation. What I place on the altar is the perspective of a trained literary critic, who happens to be a Mormon, on one of the Bible's most difficult books, which happens to be a poem.

On a few occasions in this book I will make arguments that rely on the Hebrew source text. I only do so when convinced that I am citing the near-unanimous opinions of the many excellent scholars who have spent much of their lives working with the Hebrew texts. I owe an especially strong debt to Marvin Pope's *Anchor Bible* edition of Job (1965), Carol A. Newsom's scholarly masterpiece *The Book of Job: A Contest of Moral Imaginations* (2003), Robert Alter's recent translation and commentary in *The Wisdom Books* (2010), Rabbi Harold Kushner's compulsively readable *The Book of Job: When Bad Things Happened to a Good Person* (2012), and Mark Larrimore's endlessly fascinating *The Book of Job: A Biography* (2013). The rich portraits of Job that these scholars have drawn have been a genuine pleasure to read and grapple with.

Perhaps the hardest thing that I had to do in writing this book was to choose a translation of Job to cite. The only thing that I knew for sure when I began was that I would not use the King James Version. I do not say this lightly. For the first thirty years of my life, the King James Bible was the only Bible I knew. I read it first as a practicing Latter-day Saint using the only English Bible approved by the Church, and later as a scholar of the seventeenth-century, whose literature was more influenced by this version of the Bible than by any other text, ancient or modern.

I still believe that the King James Bible is a wonderful work of literature in its own right and that it is good for many things, but understanding Job is not one of them. Unlike every other commonly available

English-language Bible, the KJV does not make any distinction between prose and poetry. It prints every line of the Bible as prose, and it elevates the diction of every sentence to the level of poetry. For all of its considerable charm, this translation strategy creates big problems for a book like Job, which switches back and forth between pedestrian prose and elevated poetry in ways that readers are supposed to notice.

As I auditioned translations, I looked for four things: 1) scholarly reliability, 2) wide availability, 3) respect for the structural and semantic parallelism of the original Hebrew verse, and 4) competent English poetry. Some translations do much better in some of these categories than others, but the one that, in my opinion, scores highest overall is the Jewish Publication Society's *Tanakh*, or simply the "JPS" (sometimes called NJPS to distinguish it from a 1917 translation by the same organization). This original translation of the Hebrew Masoretic Text involved forty Jewish scholars and rabbis over more than twenty years, culminating in its final publication in 1985. All of my citations from Job will come from this version as will nearly all other citations from the other books of the Old Testament. When referencing the New Testament, I will use the familiar King James translation. And in one place I use the *Anchor Bible* translation of a verse from Proverbs because I really like the way it reads. A foolish consistency, after all, is the hobgoblin of little minds.

As my title suggests, this is a book about how to *re-read* Job. My interpretations of the text assume that readers will have some familiarity with the story and will know the basics of the plot. But Job is probably the easiest book in the entire Bible to read badly. Because of its unique construction—beginning with a simple prose tale and continuing with an excruciatingly complicated series of poetic speeches—readers can piece together a fairly coherent narrative from the introduction and the conclusion without really understanding the very important middle. I will not try to deconstruct, reconstruct, historicize, problematize, or psychoanalyze Job in any way. I have set for myself the much more modest task of reading a difficult poem and trying to figure out what it means. This is the only service that literary critics really have to offer.

I have arranged the chapters of this book to reflect, more or less, the chronology of my own experience with the Book of Job. The first two chapters talk generally about the nature of Job and the challenge of reading scripture that is also poetry. The next four chapters provide in-depth readings of the four major divisions of the poem. Chapter Three treats the prose narrative that begins and ends the Book of Job; Chapter Four explores the dialogue between Job and his Comforters; Chapter Five deals with the Hymn to Wisdom, Job's final speech, and the speeches of Elihu; and Chapter Six tries to make sense of God's cryptic answer to Job from the whirlwind. The last four chapters of *Re-reading Job* address four of the most common lenses that people in the past have used to read and interpret Job: as a critique of Deuteronomistic orthodoxy, as an anticipation of Christianity, as a theodicy, and as an example of Wisdom literature.

A number of people read early drafts and portions of the book and offered me valuable feedback along the way. I am especially grateful to David Bokovoy and Julie Smith, who previewed *Re-reading Job* for Greg Kofford books and to Kofford's own Loyd Ericson, who took a chance on this project when it was only the barest outline of an idea. David Yee read the entire manuscript and checked each biblical quotation against the original, giving me the benefit of his careful eye and deep experience with the Tanakh. Jim Fleetwood read multiple drafts and provided valuable feedback during the writing, as did my father, Roger Austin, who first taught me to be curious about the stories of the Bible. And most of all, my wife and life partner Karen Austin read every word of the manuscript carefully, copyedited it brilliantly, and provided intellectual and emotional support during the entire project. This book would not exist without her.

My final thanks go out to the many great minds who have struggled with Job over the past 2,500 years. In each chapter, I will combine my own observations with those of these much greater writers and thinkers who have interpreted or reimagined Job through the centuries. The many novels, plays, poems, sermons, and philosophical treatises based on Job all illuminate different aspects of the text worth paying attention to. Ultimately, of course, I must bear full responsibility for the way that I have chosen to present one of the greatest works of literature ever written—and this includes owning up to any errors that I make along the way. Albert Camus once remarked that, "after a certain age every man is responsible for his face." Alas, the same holds true for one's ideas, one's opinions, and one's interpretations of Job.

A Brief Guide to Job

Prose Frame (Prologue): 1–2

The Wisdom Dialogue: 3–27

Job's Initial Speech: 3
Eliphaz's First Speech: 4–5
Job's Response: 6–7

Bildad's First Speech: 8
Job's Response: 9–10

Zophar's First Speech: 11
Job's Response: 12–14

Eliphaz's Second Speech: 15
Job's Response: 16–17

Bildad's Second Speech: 18
Job's Response: 19

Zophar's Second Speech: 20
Job's Response: 21

Eliphaz's Third Speech: 22
Job's Response: 23–24

Bildad's Third Speech: 25
Job's Response: 26–27

(Zophar does not give a third speech)

The Hymn to Wisdom: 28

Job's Final Speech: 29–31

The Speeches of Elihu: 32–37

God's Answer to Job: 38–42:6

God's First Speech: 38–40:2
Job's Response: 40:3–5

God's Second Speech: 40:6–41:26
Job's Response: 42:1–6

Prose Frame (Epilogue): 42:7–17

Chapter One

Six Things I Used to Know about Job

*Anyone interested in both the Bible and literature will eventually
find himself revolving around the Book of Job like a satellite.*
— Northrup Frye, *Words with Power*

Learning the Lessons

I first read Job in 1980 or 1981. I was in ninth grade, and our rural
Oklahoma ward wasn't big enough for early-morning seminary. There
were only four or five of us scattered across just as many small towns and
school districts, so we had a home-study course that met every week on
Sunday. But once in a while, we would all get together for a Friday-night
read-a-thon at the teacher's house. We would bring pillows and pajamas,
the teacher would have pizza, and we would read the scriptures from seven
at night until everybody fell asleep. On one such night we all read Job and
a few other books from the Old Testament. But mainly I slept.

I didn't do much better the second time through, though I have clearer memories of what I did not understand. It was in 1986, and I was an
LDS missionary in Stockton, California. I had made a goal that year to
read the entire Old Testament during my personal study time. Like any
good reader, I started at Genesis and just plowed my way through to the
end. I remember coming to the Book of Job in the text, understanding the
first few chapters quite clearly, and then passing my glazed eyes over the
complicated words and sentences that followed, assuming that they must
be saying something consistent with the chapters that had seemed so clear.

The third time I read Job was in 1988. I was a sophomore at BYU and
had just changed my major to English. My Old Testament class that semes-
ter assigned only a small portion of the Book of Job: the first two chapters,
the last half of the last chapter, and a few reputedly Christological verses

in between. But I (being a new English major and all) dutifully read the whole book, along with the analysis in the Institute Manual that we used as our text. That year, I learned more about Job than I had ever known. I learned, in fact, six concrete things that would constitute the whole of my knowledge about the Book of Job for the next ten years. Here are the six things that I learned about Job:

1. Job was a historical figure, thus the Book of Job should be read historically.
2. The Book of Job is a single, internally consistent narrative with a beginning, a middle, and an end.
3. Job was a patient fellow.
4. The Book of Job fits logically with the narrative arc of the Old Testament and with the other Standard Works.
5. In the midst of his great suffering, Job occasionally, and for no apparent reason, prophesied of Christ with famous words like "I know that my Redeemer lives."
6. The Book of Job ultimately shows that, if we just wait long enough, God will reward our good behavior with material prosperity.

I knew, in other words, that part of Job that one can learn by reading the first two chapters, the last half of the last chapter, and a few reputedly Christological verses in between.

I did not read Job again in graduate school, even though I ended up writing a dissertation on the ways that seventeenth-century poets (Milton, Dryden, Cowley, etc.) understood the Old Testament in their poetry. But I did read hundreds of books and articles on the literary motifs of the Hebrew Bible. I published articles on Genesis, Samuel, Ruth, and the Psalms in respectable journals with rigorous standards for peer review. And somehow I managed to do all of this without ever learning the most basic and obvious fact about the Book of Job: it—or at least most of it—is a poem.

But even overspecialized new Ph.D.'s can't go on knowing nothing forever. When I landed my first teaching job at a state university in West Virginia, half of my teaching load was in a general-education world literature class that every student in the college had to take. All sections of the class used the *Norton Anthology of World Literature*. Everybody had to teach Job. I was not worried; I was an expert, after all, and I knew six things about Job. But when I read the headnote in the Norton anthology, I realized very quickly that I'd been had. My previous assumptions about the Book of Job were not merely wrong; they were spectacularly wrong. I had no business trying to teach anybody about the greatest literary work of the Bible. And that day in the fall of 1997, I began the painful process of unlearning everything I knew about the Book of Job.

Unlearning the Lessons

The Book of Job challenges its readers more than most books of the Bible do, but the challenges are not insurmountable. Job is certainly no more difficult than most of William Faulkner's novels, and it is nowhere near as hard as *Ulysses* or *Finnegan's Wake* by James Joyce. By the third time that I read Job, I had already learned how to read and understand considerably more difficult works of literature. But I knew that those books were going to be hard. When I read *Ulysses* in college, for example, I had no illusions about breezing through it in a few days. I read it at a desk with Stuart Gilbert's commentary always on the left and Don Gifford's independent annotations always on the right. I got a lot out of it only because I put a lot into it, which is generally how most of us non-geniuses have to read difficult things.

But I never thought that I needed help understanding Job. In the first place, I always read it as part of a larger text—the Christian Bible—which provided much of my narrative framework for understanding it. I was thirty years old before it ever occurred to me to read Job as a book in its own right and not as a small chapter in a much larger drama involving chosen people, golden calves, sin, destruction, apples, nakedness, and the coming of a Messiah to atone for our sins. This context severely constrains the ways that we can read Job and all but eliminates the possibility of reading it as a critique of other books in the Bible.

But the hardest thing about the Book of Job, at least in my experience, is that it does not start out being hard. Both the beginning and the end of Job read like a children's story, and these are the parts where everything seems to happen. The thirty-nine hard chapters come in the middle, which just looks like a lot of introspection and navel gazing. Our training as readers tells us that, as long as we understand the beginning and the end of a story, we can fake it through the middle just assuming that it more or less follows a trajectory that we can derive from the end points. In most cases, this strategy will work just fine—but not in Job. The Book of Job's unique construction makes it impossible to understand the middle of the story by simply extrapolating from the beginning and the end.

At the heart of the difficulty lies the fact that the Book of Job contains two fundamentally incompatible stories about a man named Job. The first Job story, which predates the biblical book by as much as 500 years, was a common Near Eastern folk tale about a guy who loses everything yet never complains to his god. The second Job story is a Hebrew poem that challenges many of the assumptions of the folk tale by having its supposedly complacent hero abandon all pretense of patience and complain, in excruciating detail, about his god.

Here is how I usually explain the two Jobs to my students: imagine a written version of the Cinderella story that begins and ends with a simple paraphrase of the Disney movie but contains, in between, a 10,000 word poem called "Cinderella's Lament"—a brilliantly written feminist manifesto challenging most of the sexist assumptions in the original story. Imagine that the poem is written primarily from Cinderella's perspective but includes speeches by the stepmother and stepsisters as well.

The Cinderella of the poem (let us imagine) is as radical as the Disney version is safe. She questions some of her culture's deepest values and beliefs that women should marry men, that rich and handsome princes are automatically desirable, that a man can love a woman even if he can't remember what she looks like. The other characters in the poem are, of course, horrified by her unorthodox views, and they do everything they can to contradict her. Every time she speaks, they rebut everything she says. But Cinderella is a clever debater, and she holds her own.

They go on arguing and arguing until the Fairy Godmother shows up and angrily puts an end to the debate. "I spent a lot of time and effort catching you a prince," she tells Cinderella, "and you had better marry him fast if you don't want to end up a pumpkin yourself." Cinderella knows when she has been beaten, and she submits—not to a better argument, but to superior physical force. She marries the prince, and they live happily ever after—except, of course, they don't, and we know they don't because we have been made privy to Cinderella's deepest thoughts. This is roughly how the Book of Job would have looked to its first generation of readers. As modern readers, of course, we can never experience Job this way because we have never encountered one of the stories without the other. The only text that we have stitches the two Jobs together. But we can see the seams. And to understand the Book of Job in any but the most superficial sense, we must acknowledge those seams and understand that somebody put them together for a reason. Once we understand the reason, we can make some pretty good guesses about the meaning of the poem.

It is with this in mind that I offer the following revisions to the six things that I used to know about Job:

1. **Job is a highly stylized work of imaginative literature that may or may not have been based on the experiences of a real person but cannot be considered objective history.**

    Everything about the Book of Job announces that it is a work of literature. It begins with the Hebrew equivalent of "once upon a time" and deliberately steers us away from any historical place or period. It features immortal characters (God and Satan) acting in ways that are inconsistent with their actions anywhere else in the Bible. It contains several different kinds of writing, but much of it is written in what competent scholars consider the most formally excellent Hebrew poetry found anywhere.

    This does not mean that there was never a man named something like "Job" who had a lot of stuff, lost it all, and then got it back again. There certainly could have been—just as there could have been a man named Odysseus who got lost on the way home from a war. But it would be just as incorrect to read Job as the actual history of a wealthy man of the East as it would be to read the *Odyssey* as a first-person account of a journey. When we try to turn an obvious work of literature into a historical record, we end up asking the wrong kinds of questions, and, in turn, learning the wrong kinds of lessons.

    One of my primary arguments here is that written texts "want" to be read in certain ways. This is of course an oversimplification. Clearly, inanimate objects such as poems and history books don't really have desires. But authors have intentions, and, invariably they leave clues in their texts about how they expect those texts to be read. We are pretty good at reading these clues in books from our own culture. If a work begins with "once upon a time," we know that it will probably be either a fairy tale or a satire of a fairy tale. If it has seventeen syllables and talks about cherry blossoms, then we can be pretty sure that it is a haiku.

    With a book like Job, however, we no longer have access to all of the cultural assumptions that were shared by its author and its original readers. And this means that we can easily miss the clues and genre markers that tell us how we should read it. Furthermore, most people today encounter Job as part of a larger work that we have been trained to read in very specific ways. When we encounter the Book of Job in the Bible, we very naturally want to read it the same way we read the Book of Exodus or the Book of Judges.

We should remember, however, that the Bible is not as much of a book as it is a library—and what we call the Old Testament contains the most significant writings of an entire ancient culture. Like any good library, the Old Testament contains history books and instruction manuals. It contains overtly religious works that declare the mind of God directly through prophecy, and it also contains magnificent works of literature that teach spiritual truths imaginatively, through poetry and narrative. We owe it to the writers of all of these books to learn the differences between them and to read each book the way that it asks to be read.

2.   **The Book of Job contains two basic parts: a simplistic prose frame and a complicated long poem, with the latter designed to comment ironically on the former.**

The Job frame, which consists of chapters 1–2 and 42:7–16, tells the tale of a righteous man who suffers extreme misfortunes, endures them all with patience and faith, and gets rewarded handsomely in the end for being such a good sport. This story, it turns out, is much older than our Book of Job—perhaps as much as 500 or more years older. Scholars have found traces of this story throughout the Ancient Near East, among Akkadians, Babylonians, Hittites, and many more.[1]

The Job poet positions the poem as a challenge to the simplistic ideology of the folk tale. The Job of the poem complains loudly, to anyone who will listen, that God has treated him unfairly. The more his friends try to defend God, the more they feel that they have to blame Job for his own suffering, and the angrier he gets. Using the Ancient Near Eastern literary form known as a "Wisdom dialogue," the poet explores, and rejects, his culture's most common explanations for human suffering.

The relationship between the poem and the frame is almost entirely ironic. The poem works precisely because it requires us to discount the Job of the frame in favor of the more fully realized Job of the poem. But we are not used to dealing with this level of irony in the Bible, nor do we expect to find admirable characters questioning God's morality. The Job poem is hard to read, and it says things that

---

1. Mark Larrimore, *The Book of Job: A Biography*, 16, 40–49; Samuel Terrien, *Job: The Poet of Existence*, 28–29.

make us uncomfortable. The Job frame, on the other hand, is simple, easy to understand, and it says the kinds of things that we think the Bible is supposed to say.

Modern readers, therefore, tend to read Job like this: we read and understand the first two chapters without any problem, and then, when we hit the hard stuff in chapter 3, we start skimming. Since we assume that we have a handle on the story, we miss the enormity of the transition from the frame to the poem and simply assume that it works like most of the narratives we know, with the middle flowing logically from the beginning. We skip over the most difficult passages because we are fairly sure that we know what they say, and, when we get to the end, we see that everything worked out like we thought it would.

As the twentieth-century theologian Samuel Terrien describes, we come to the poem "vaguely acquainted with the story of a man of faith." Therefore, "we usually ignore the poem of his doubt. Remembering the plot of the folk tale in prose, we too often neglect the dialogue in verse. Yet, the poetic discourses are the *raison d'etre* of the book, and the popular narrative that surrounds them is only the occasion of the poem."[2] And in this way, one of the most profound parts of the Bible has remained hidden in plain sight for more than 2,000 years.

3. **The much-lauded "patience of Job" ends with chapter 2, after which Job complains almost constantly about God.**

The phrase "the patience of Job" has become idiomatic among people who have never opened a Bible. Religious materials often collaborate to reinforce this reading by ignoring virtually all of the poem and focusing on the lessons of the frame. This ensures that the Book of Job says the sorts of thing that Bible stories are supposed to say. It tells us to worship God in good times and bad—and it warns us against forsaking God and "sinning with our lips." It gives us a great example of a man who loses everything and remains steadfast—and who is rewarded in the end for his patience and his faith. And it allows us to comfort (but really to criticize) those who are complaining about something in their own lives with the allegedly cheery thought that, at least, they aren't as bad off as Job.

Who would want to muck up this perfectly wonderful little object lesson with a 10,000-word poem complaining bitterly about God's injustice? But that is what follows the second chapter. At the

---

2. Terrien, *Job: The Poet of Existence*, 23.

very beginning of chapter 3, Job himself immediately gives lie to the "Patient Job" narrative by cursing—roughly in order—the day he was born, the night he was conceived, his mother's womb, the knees that received him, and the breasts that gave him suck. And then he starts questioning the justice of God so fiercely that his friends feel compelled to break their silence and defend the Almighty.

4. **The Job poem powerfully critiques much of the Old Testament's internal logic.**

The Old Testament histories were designed to explain how the Jews went from the glories of David and Solomon to their humiliating captivity in Babylon after the destruction of Jerusalem in 587 B.C. This was the most important question that the post-exilic Jewish community—which compiled and constructed the documents that we now call the Old Testament—could ask.[3] And their answer was remarkable: God did not abandon us, they reasoned, we abandoned God. Despite Moses's clear warnings in Deuteronomy, we rejected Him and chased after false gods. The fact that we have been punished so severely demonstrates the severity of our sins.

The Book of Job is a dissenting opinion from this party line. Rather than trying to defend the Jews, or argue that they have not sinned against God, the Job poet directly attacks the major premise of his culture's most powerful syllogism. The fact of punishment, he argues, is not an evidence of sin. This is the point that Job makes over and over again to his interlocutors—and it is the point that they stubbornly refuse to consider. But really, they can't consider it without undermining one of the core beliefs through which they make sense of the world. Rather than go through the difficult work of revising their worldview, Job's Comforters abandon their compassion for their suffering friend and become his tormentors—and this, too, is part of the poet's critique.

The Job poet dared to critique, and dismantle, the most powerful religious orthodoxy of his culture by confronting it with a set of facts that it could not accommodate. And he demonstrated in excruciating detail how those who hold to rigid orthodoxies will end up renouncing both overwhelming evidence and basic human decency before abandoning their beliefs.

---

3. For an introduction to the composition of the Old Testament, see David Bokovoy's *Authoring the Old Testament* series.

5. **When Job speaks of a "Redeemer," he is not prophesying of Christ. He is invoking his right to an avenger.**

    In every Church lesson that I have ever had about the Book of Job we have read the twenty-fifth verse of chapter 19: "For I know *that* my redeemer liveth, and *that* he shall stand at the latter *day* upon the earth" (KJV). What clearer evidence could we have of Job's faith, not just in God, but in Jesus Christ, who would not be born for at least another 500 years? Samuel Medley's 1775 poem "I Know that My Redeemer Lives" has been set to music many times and is, in one of its versions, one of the most cherished songs in the LDS hymnal. Other denominations use a hymn of the same name written by Charles Wesley or the version from George Frideric Handel's famous oratorio, *Messiah*.

    Unfortunately, there is no way to read the original text as a prophecy of Christ. The Hebrew root word that Job uses here (and which Christian translators have long translated as "Redeemer") is *ga'al*, which means something more like "avenger" or "reputation fixer." This was someone who had the charge to preserve the reputation of a deceased family member. The role of a *ga'al* varied widely depending on the circumstances. It could require someone to avenge a death with bloodshed or to provide evidence exonerating somebody who died under a cloud of suspicion. But it could also include marrying a deceased man's wife and siring children in his name—as Boaz did with Ruth, acting in his role as *ga'al*.

    It is possible, of course, to see in the Hebrew *ga'al* a figuration of the role of Jesus Christ. It is not possible, however, to actually agree with Job in thinking that a *ga'al*, or redeemer, will some day confront God and prove his innocence. This would require us to accept the proposition that Job's suffering is connected to his behavior—that God is actually punishing him for supposedly doing something wrong. And this is precisely the proposition that the whole poem is trying to convince us to reject. The fact that Job believes that his "Redeemer lives" shows us that, at this point in the poem, he has no more ability than his friends to comprehend a God who does not operate on a straightforward principle of rewards and punishments.

6. **The finale of Job, in which he is richly rewarded for his faithfulness, is part of the frame, not the poem, which means that it is part of what the author is trying to undercut.**

The traditional Job story ends with God restoring Job's health and doubling his property. If we take this as the ultimate meaning of the Book of Job, we will end up reinstating all of the assumptions about rewards and punishments that the poet worked so hard to get us to reject. It is crucial, therefore, that we understand that this final scene is part of the frame tale, not the poem, and that one of the most important functions of the poem is to question the ideology of the frame.

Keep in mind that most of the original readers would have known the Job story and would be expecting the big reward at the end. If the poet has done his job, however, the ending should fall flat. We should realize that the version of God that we see in the frame is nothing like the version that we see in the poem, and that the idea of rewarding somebody who has suffered patiently (or even impatiently) flies in the face of the poem's more nuanced and spiritually mature understanding of God. We should, in other words, read the final verses of Job ironically.

Let me be very clear here about what I am not saying. I do not suggest that some hapless editor joined the frame and the poem together because he didn't understand how different they were. Nor do I think (as some have argued) that a pious redactor, centuries after the poem was written, slapped on the last few verses to blunt the original critique. Rather, I accept what has become the predominant (but by no means unanimous) view of scholars: the author of the Book of Job knew exactly what he was doing when he juxtaposed the frame and the poem, and he clearly intended us to read the frame, including the final scene, ironically.

The book that I have outlined above is not the Book of Job that most Latter-day Saints encounter in their Gospel Doctrine, Seminary, and Institute classes. We are not alone here. Most religious commentary presents Job as an exemplar of patience and faithfulness and has for thousands of years. We don't really need to think very hard about why. "Complaining Job" isn't much of a role model. Nobody wants to cut out flannel board pictures of a man shaking his fist at God or put students in small groups to talk about the last time they tried to obliterate the day of their conception. As long as the designers of religious curricula use the scriptures to reinforce desired behaviors, they are always going to gravitate toward the patient fellow in the Job folk tale—and to the man of faith who knew that his Redeemer lived.

Read properly, the Book of Job is not the sort of thing that one would want to use to reinforce religious orthodoxies. It is an extremely subversive work of literature. It challenges assumptions about God, morality, and justice that have been central to human religious thought for millennia and remain so today. And it is especially hard on orthodox religious beliefs. It has long been in the interest of institutional religions to try to contain the more radical implications of the Job poem by focusing, whenever possible, on the jaunty, pious tale that introduces it.

Asking the Right Questions

In this book, I treat Job as a work of imaginative literature, which, I believe, is an essential starting point for responsible interpretation. To wrest meaningful answers from any complex work, we must start with meaningful questions. If we insist on reading Job as a historical narrative, with the first two chapters carrying the bulk of the history, we will have a very difficult time coming up with any good questions at all. We will be too busy trying to solve the serious theological problems that these first two chapters, if read historically, raise. Seen as the actual interactions between God and a historical person, Job alternates between the horrific and the absurd. In the first two chapters, God invites his archenemy up to heaven for a chat and then offers up Job as an example of a truly righteous man. To score a few debating points, God allows Satan to kill this man's children and inflict him with grievous suffering just to see if it will make him crack.

The end of the Job poem is even more problematic than the beginning. When Job finishes kvetching, God appears in the form of a whirlwind to tell Job how powerful he is and how puny Job and his friends are. The God of Job does not act like the vindictive God of the Old Testament or the merciful God of the New Testament. Rather, He acts like a neurotic playground bully shaking Job down for his lunch money. For this portrayal to make any sense at all as a historical record, we must frame the narrative in a way that prevents it from making sense as anything else. And this, in turn, requires us to ask, and to try to answer, a lot of difficult questions that don't actually matter very much to the points that the author wants to make. Does God really make friendly bets with Satan? Why would a just God kill a man's children in order to score debating points? Was Job tested beyond what a human being can endure? When does the action in Job occur? Why did God bother to appear to Job in the first place if He wasn't going to answer his questions? And just where is the Land of Uz? These are the sorts of questions that we have to ask if we consider Job a historical text. They are precisely the wrong questions to ask if we are trying to derive any kind of meaning from a work of literature. When we shift our assumptions just a little bit and allow the Book of Job to be what it claims to be, we find ourselves able to ask much better questions of the text—the questions that can give us the kinds of answers that can change our lives. In Job, such questions might include the following:

- Why did the best Jewish poet of the post-exile generation choose the (probably) Persian fable of Job as the basis for his greatest work?
- What does the obviously Hebrew poet want to accomplish by presenting Job as an "Everyman" character rather than as a Jew? What does this suggest about the way that the Abrahamic Covenant was understood by at least some people during the Babylonian captivity?
- What different perspectives do Job's Comforters represent? Who in the poet's culture held the views attributed to Eliphaz, Bildad, and Zophar?
- Why do Job's friends hold so firmly to their belief in Job's guilt? Why are they willing to condemn the man that they came to comfort? What do they consider more important than friendship? Do we ever act like they do?
- How does the poet want us to answer the question, "Why do people suffer?" How does he not want us to answer this question?
- Why does the poet represent God at the end of Job as an asker of questions rather than as a giver of answers? Does the God that the poet presents at the end of the poem deserve our respect, or just our fear? Is there a difference?
- Does the final prose segment of Job undercut the poem? Or does the poem's rebuttal undercut its ideology so effectively that it becomes ironic? Is it possible to believe in a God of rewards and punishments after reading Job?

These are the kinds of questions that matter when we are reading Job because they are the kinds of questions that can lead us to meaningful reflections about important human concerns. Every minute that we spend trying to figure out whether the "Leviathan" mentioned in chapter 42 is an ancient sea monster or just a plain old crocodile takes us further away from the book's most profound truths. If we can give ourselves permission to understand Job as something other than reliable, documentary history, then we can get down to the really important business of understanding how it is true as a poem.

The Ancient World's Greatest Poem?

Unlearning is a painful process because it requires humility, recognition of past errors, and the persistent suspicion that, having been wrong once, one could easily be wrong again. I once knew six things about Job with great confidence. Now I suspect six very different things about Job that, I realize, could easily turn out to be wrong. But when I read Job according to the things I suspect, rather than the things I used to know, I can see why people like Victor Hugo and Thomas Carlyle called the Book of Job the world's greatest literary work.

I am not quite prepared to follow Hugo or Carlyle in labeling Job the best thing ever written. But I am quite comfortable calling it—as I have called it in the subtitle of this book—"the ancient world's greatest poem." This is no small praise, as it vaults it ahead of some very important works, such as the *Iliad* and the *Odyssey* of Homer, Virgil's *Aeneid*, and Ovid's *Metamorphoses*—not to mention some of the greatest classics of the Eastern world, like the *Ramayana*, the *Mahabharata*, and the *Tao te Ching*. I have deep respect for these works, as I do for the tragedies of Aeschylus and Euripides, the satires of Horace and Juvenal, and the other great poetic works of the Hebrew Bible. But I have no hesitation praising Job above them all.

It is not the profundity of his suffering that makes Job unique. Pound for pound, nobody did suffering better than the Greeks, and they were very good at using profound suffering to showcase the depths of human emotion. For all of Job's trials, he at least never stabs his eyes out after killing his father and marrying his mother, nor does God chain him to a rock and send an eagle every day to devour his perpetually regenerating liver. Oedipus and Prometheus could teach Job a thing or two about human misery.

But only Job struggles to make moral sense of his suffering. When Greek heroes suffer, they shake their fist at the gods and demand respect, but only Job shakes his fist at God and demands justice. When Roman heroes find their friends recalcitrant, they require rectitude and obedience, but only Job has the audacity to require compassion. And, unlike any other literary hero of the ancient world, Job has the courage to stare straight into the face of a seemingly arbitrary cosmos and demand that the universe make sense.

In many respects, the "big question" usually attributed to the Book of Job—"why do bad things happen to good people?"—is one of the least interesting things about it. The poet asks much more interesting questions than this—questions like "how can we keep from being miserable in a universe that we can neither predict nor control?" "why do the ideological structures that we create to help us understand the world end up preventing us from acting effectively in it?" and "what is our moral responsibility to other people whom we believe to be wrong, but who desperately need our support and affection?"

These are not easy questions, but they are questions that human beings still ask. They are not unique to any religious or cultural perspectives. Modern existentialists and secular humanists ask these questions just as frequently, and just as profoundly, as Ancient Jews or Medieval Christians. The Jewish writer Cynthia Ozick, I think, gets it exactly right when she writes that "like almost no other primordial poem the West has inherited, the Book of Job is conceived under the aspect of the universal—if the universal is understood to be a questioning so organic to our nature that no creed or philosophy can elude it."[4]

And yet a huge number of religious people still see Job as an affirming story about a guy who endures a lot of trials without complaining—and is rewarded in the end for his great faithfulness. Millions of people know Job only as the story of the frame. This confusion has been around for a long time, of course, and it may very well have helped the Book of Job make it into the Bible to begin with. But the same things that have made the Job frame so famous have also kept people from trying to understand the rest of it. As a result, readers have been reading Job badly—and missing the main points of its remarkable creator—for a very, very long time.

This is why unlearning things about Job is so important. When we approach a difficult book that we know nothing about, we usually take some steps to learn about it before we begin and understand it better while we read. But when we read a book that we think we already understand, we immediately fit everything we read into the understanding that we already possess. This works pretty well until we encounter a book whose author wants us to question everything that we think we already know and to go even further and question our assumptions about what it means to know things.

In the following chapters, I hope that I will be able to convince you that Job is precisely such a book.

---

4. Cynthia Ozick, "The Impious Impatience of Job," 15.

Chapter Two

Job as History / Job as Literature

"Out of the quarrel with others we make rhetoric; out of the quarrel with ourselves, poetry." —William Butler Yeats

The Quest for the Historical Job

Did a man named Job ever live? A great many people—many of them Latter-day Saints—believe this to be an extremely important question. Often this comes from a reflexive biblical literalism that we inherited from our Protestant forbearers. Like our Evangelical cousins, Latter-day Saints tend to be uncomfortable thinking of any part of the Bible as imaginative literature—under the assumption that this would decrease its moral value and call the legitimacy of the entire biblical narrative into question.

Latter-day Saints have less reason than most to think this way. Mormons do not and cannot accept the doctrine of biblical literalism as understood by much of the Christian world. Joseph Smith closed this door forever when he produced his Inspired Version of the Bible that, among other things, added lengthy passages to Genesis and Matthew, emended multiple passages with no reference to the primary texts, and declared one canonical book—the Song of Solomon—"not inspired." No biblical literalist could accept such innovations.

Even so, however, Mormon readers often insist on the historicity of Job because references to the Book of Job appear in other scriptures. The passage in Doctrine and Covenants 121:10—in which God comforts Joseph Smith in Liberty Jail by telling him, "Thou art not yet as Job"—has been particularly compelling evidence of Job's historicity for Latter-day Saints. For example, the LDS institute manual places a substantial portion of its commentary on Job under the heading, "Was Job a Real Person?" To answer this question, the manual reprints portions of an address by BYU religion professor Keith H. Meservy:

Now, if Job were not real and his suffering, therefore, were merely the fig-
ment of some author's imagination, and Joseph Smith on the other hand was
very real, and his suffering and that of his people were not imaginary, then
for the Lord to chide him because his circumstances were not as bad as Job's
were, would provide an intolerable comparison, since one cannot compare
real with unreal things. On the other hand, since the Lord did make the
comparison, it must be a real one. I would, therefore, conclude on this basis
alone, that Job was a very real person.[1]

I see two legitimate objections to this position. In the first place, it is
not at all obvious to me that "one cannot compare real with unreal things"
or that the circumstances of a real person cannot be compared productive-
ly to those of a literary creation. During his earthly ministry, Jesus made
such comparisons frequently by answering real people's concerns with in-
structional parables. Modern prophets and apostles frequently refer to the
Good Samaritan or the Prodigal Son in conference talks, even though they
know perfectly well that these figures never existed. Literary parables have
long been able to serve an important role in prophetic teaching without
staking any kind of historical claim.

It is entirely possible, of course, that a man named Job did actually
live, suffer greatly, and remain steadfast in his testimony of God. Even if
we grant all of this, however, it still does not follow that we should read
the Book of Job as documentary history. Many of the world's greatest
poems have some basis in the lives of historical figures, but this does not
make them historical texts. *The Epic of Gilgamesh, Faust, El Cid, The Song
of Roland, Sundiata,* and *Richard III* are all stories of people who actually
lived, but they are also all works of art and can only be read profitably as
such. *The Song of Roland,* for example, gives very little accurate historical
information about the Battle of Roncesvalles. It does, though, tell us a
great deal about the state of French nationalism in the late Middle Ages.
And none of this means that there was no Charlemagne.

Even if there were a historical Job who left an accurate record of his
life, we cannot be certain that the version in our Bible is that record. There
were other versions of the story floating around the ancient world. In the
most famous of these, "The Testament of Job," a man named "Jobab"
suffers greatly after he destroys one of Satan's Egyptian shrines, but he
remains patient and is eventually rescued by God. When this version is
compared to other extant ancient texts, biblical scholar Mark Larrimore
writes, we find that "these versions of the Job story . . . are more like each

---

1. *Old Testament Student Manual 1 Kings–Malachi,* 28–29.

other than the canonical text" and that "it was this tradition, rather than the canonical text, to which the epistle of James refers when it assumes that its readers will have 'heard of the patience of Job'" (5:11).[2]

Latter-day Saints are not alone in insisting on a historical Job, of course. For millennia, Christian commentators have been tying themselves in logical and theological knots trying to make the Book of Job into good history. But making spiritual points by telling stories and writing poems has always been an essential part of the Jewish tradition. This is why even the earliest Talmudic scholars were comfortable with the notion that "Job never was and never existed, but is only a typical figure."[3] And it is why the great twelfth-century Jewish philosopher Moses Maimonides had no qualms about declaring Job "a fiction, conceived for the purpose of explaining the different opinions which people hold on Divine Providence."[4] The Jewish tradition, which gave us the Book of Job, has long understood it as a religious allegory rather than a spiritual history.

Had Job's original readers understood it as history or prophecy, they would have put it in a very different place than they did when they compiled their first anthology of sacred texts. The Hebrew *Tanakh*—which Christians now call the "Old Testament"—consists of a few key legal and historical documents (*Torah*), a large number of works considered prophetic (*Nevi'im*), and a collection of "writings" (*Kethuvim*) comprised of poems (Psalms, the Song of Songs, Lamentations), prose tales (Esther, Ruth), wisdom sayings (Proverbs, Ecclesiastes), and the Book of Job. I suspect that Job's original readers (and hearers) would not have understood why anybody would insist on it being factual history. They knew perfectly well that it was not—which is why they put it in the "literature" section of the *Tanakh* to begin with.

Though the question of Job's historicity has never been the subject of specific revelation for Latter-day Saints, it has been the subject of at least one semi-official letter from a First Presidency source, as Thomas Alexander reports in *Mormonism in Transition*:

> In October 1922, while Heber J. Grant was in Washington, the First Presidency received a letter from Joseph W. McMurrin asking about the position of the Church with regard to the literality of the Bible. Charles W. Penrose, with Anthony W. Ivins, writing for the First Presidency, answered that the position of the Church was that the Bible is the word of God as far

---

2. Mark Larrimore, *The Book of Job: A Biography*, 41.

3. Ibid., 57.

4. Moses Maimonides, *The Guide for the Perplexed*, 296.

as it was translated correctly. They pointed out that there were, however, some problems with the Old Testament. . . . While they thought Jonah was a real person, they said it was possible that the story as told in the Bible was a parable common at the time. The purpose was to teach a lesson, and it "is of little significance as to whether Jonah was a real individual or one chosen by the writer of the book" to illustrate "what is set forth therein." They took a similar position on Job.[5]

As the Higher Criticism controversy raged around them, the LDS First Presidency's position on the Book of Job was threefold: 1) that its author was inspired, 2) that its message is true, and 3) that it is "of little significance" to the truth of the scriptural narrative whether we see Job as a history or as a parable. In a 1990 article, former BYU Provost John Tanner comes to the same conclusion: "One question . . . that many readers seize upon as they wrestle with the text is 'Is Job historical?' Personally, I am not persuaded that the answer to this question makes much difference for the interpretation of the text."[6]

As Latter-day Saints, in other words, we are free to seek our own inspiration in determining whether or not there was an actual man named Job who lived in a place called Uz. Like Professor Tanner, I do not believe that the answer to this question matters. And even if it does matter, there is no way to settle the issue with historical or textual analysis. Those who believe in a historical Job do so for reasons of faith. Given the fog of 3,000 years or more, there is no objective way to assess the historicity of Job. A much easier question, and one that we can answer with greater objectivity, is "does the Book of Job present itself to us as a historical work?" Here, there is very little ambiguity. It does not. For its original readers, the Book of Job contained enough clear markers of its fictional status to make such a reading untenable.

For an example of what I mean, imagine that you have just picked up a dusty, old book with an unmarked cover and the following sentence on the first page:

> Once upon a time, in a faraway land, there lived a beautiful young maiden who longed for a life of adventure, a handsome young prince who longed to settle down, and a wise old woman who knew a few things about magic and a great many things about love.

---

5. Thomas Alexander, *Mormonism in Transition: A History of the Latter-day Saints, 1890-1930*, 299–300.

6. John S. Tanner, "Why Latter-Day Saints Should Read Job," 39.

You would immediately recognize that everything about the passage screams "fairy tale." It begins with the standard fairy tale marker, "once upon a time," and it uses other phrases—"faraway land," "beautiful young maiden," "life of adventure"—that would seem hopelessly out of place in a history book but right at home in any fairy tale. And it introduces fairy-tale themes, such as romance, adventure, and magic. If it is not a fairy tale, it is a text that has been designed to mimic the conventions of fairy tales, possibly to satirize them (think *The Princess Bride* or *Shrek*). No experienced reader could possibly mistake this for a work of objective history.

Ancient audiences would have recognized just as many markers of fictionality in the Book of Job. Many of these markers have faded with the passage of time, but many others remain. Scholars note that Job begins with as clear a textual marker of its fictionality as the ancient Hebrew language could provide. The first words of the original Hebrew text—*'ish hayah*, or "a man there was"—invert the normal word order for historical narratives in Hebrew (*wayehi 'ish*, or "there was a man"). The eminent Hebrew scholar Robert Alter explains that this inversion "signal[s] the fable-like character of the frame story." The best equivalent that we have in English would be "once upon a time."[7]

The Job narrative also acts like a fable in that it refuses to situate itself in time or space. It could be set anywhere in the ancient world at any time from the days before the Flood to the Babylonian captivity. The characters in Job that we are familiar with (God and Satan) act in ways that contradict everything that we know about them from other sources. And, as we have already seen, the text of Job combines two very different, often conflicting versions of the same narrative into a single book. Even allowing for the cultural differences between Ancient Hebrew culture and our own, it would be difficult to imagine a historian constructing a narrative through persistent irony, figurative language, and unstable meanings. These are the tools of the poet, and the Book of Job employs them better than nearly any other poem in the canon of world literature.

One of the main points of this book is that there is no reason that a work of imaginative literature cannot also be a work of divine revelation. We must not confuse "the facts" with "the truth." Completely verifiable facts can always be combined into narratives that produce false ideas. We call this propaganda. Conversely, acknowledged fictions can be assembled into narratives that convey profound—and true—insights to those who read them.

---

7. Robert Alter, *The Wisdom Books: Job, Proverbs, and Ecclesiastes: A Translation with Commentary*, 11.

We call this, among other things, great literature. I can see no reason that a god who wanted to say something important to human beings would hesitate to inspire somebody to write a great poem and call it scripture.

How Is Literature True?

We should never condemn a book for not being something that it does not claim to be. There are many legitimate reasons not to like Dante's *Divine Comedy*, but the fact that Dante got the physics of earth's core wrong is not one of them. *Inferno* makes strong claims to moral and allegorical truth that we are free to accept or reject. But it makes no claims to scientific truth, so to judge it on that basis misses the point of the work.

Some books in the Bible present themselves to us with strong claims to historical or prophetic truth. Some of these books take the form of poetry, such as the book of Isaiah, which presents itself as true in the "thus-sayeth-the-Lord" way of being true. But not every book in the Bible presents itself this way. Some, like Job, make the kinds of truth claims that Dante's *Inferno* makes. As readers, I believe, we should read all books—especially the scriptures—the way that they ask to be read.

So how do poems claim to be true? This is really the big question I am asking in this book. The great resistance that Latter-day Saints and others have toward calling poetic scriptures "literary" comes because this label seems to make the scriptures less true. I want to state emphatically that I do not believe this. A literary creation can be just as inspired, just as instructive, and just as true as a historical record—and it can be much more valuable. In any contest of religious or moral "truth," I would happily put the Parable of the Good Samaritan—an acknowledged fiction—up against the nineteenth chapter of Judges, which tells the historical but not terrifically inspiring story of the Levite's concubine who was raped, murdered, cut into twelve pieces, and sent to each of the tribes of Israel.[8] Just because something happened does not mean that it is morally instructive; just because it never happened does not mean that it is not true.

In the twenty years or so that I have taught literature to college students, I have had much occasion to think about how literary truth claims work. There is not a complete list or a diagram anywhere that everybody accepts. Literature works simultaneously on emotional and intellectual levels; therefore, we experience literature in ways that sterile

---

8. By calling this story "historical," I do not assert that it actually happened, but that it presents itself as historical fact which we can either accept or reject.

critical analysis can never fully explain. But literary texts do claim things. They make arguments and function as part of a rhetorical context. And they make arguments differently than other kinds of texts do. Below are a few of my own observations about the ways that literature makes and sustains truth claims.

Literature rarely places historical or scientific claims at issue

Dante didn't travel through hell. Casey never struck out. Grecian urns don't talk. For thousands of years, people have loved and learned things from poems and other works of literature that they understood as imaginative fictions. These poems are true because they lead us to valid intellectual and moral insights. Though literature often embeds information about science and history—sometimes intentionally and sometimes ironically—the truth of these embedded claims has little bearing on their primary arguments.

Consider Edgar Allen Poe's famous poem, "The Raven." Here we have a first-person narrator whose wife or lover, Lenore, has recently died. He is in his library searching through his books to find a way to make her death meaningful—or even understandable. When a raven enters the library, the narrator takes it as a sign and asks a series of increasingly desperate questions. The raven, of course, has long been a symbol for death, and the questions that the narrator asks the raven are all really questions about death. Is there a heaven? Does death come from God or the Devil? Will he ever get over her death? Will he see her again? These are likely the same things he was trying to find out from his books. But while the books may have tried to give answers, the raven—death itself—says only one word: "Nevermore."

So this is a poem that makes claims—or, more specifically, it is a poem that rejects claims. It rejects the notion that anyone can know anything about death, or what happens after death, except that a person who has died no longer exists. All that death "says" to us is "Nevermore." If we try to go beyond this, we will eventually suffer the narrator's fate and become insane. Many people would disagree vigorously with this premise. Some people believe that the spirits of the dead become ghosts that we can still communicate with. Others believe in heaven, hell, reincarnation, Nirvana, or some knowable final destination for the soul. I can imagine a number of different ways that one might go about rebutting Poe's metaphysical truth claims.

But it makes no difference whether or not ravens can talk. Nothing about Poe's poem can be supported, or refuted, by scientific knowledge about the vocalization mechanisms of the *Corvus corax*. Nor does it matter whether or not Edgar Allen Poe ever knew anybody named Lenore, or owned a "bust of Pallas," or did or said any of the things described in the poem. "The Raven" makes metaphysical truth claims that we can isolate and evaluate. But these claims do not depend on either the history or the science of the poem turning out to be true.[9]

Both the form and the content of literature contribute to its meaning

Try this experiment: imagine that somebody you love and respect greatly has died and that you have been asked to compose a brief poem to read at the funeral. The poem should be respectful, serious, somber, and should capture all of your feelings for this individual. All of the person's friends and family will be there and will be looking to you for comfort at one of the most difficult times of their lives. And one more thing: the poem has to be a limerick.

Most people can't do it. When I ask students to try, they often tell me that they can't even begin to write such a poem because it seems too disrespectful. Others come up with three or even four somber and serious lines, but they always end with a humorous zinger. No matter how hard we try, something about the limerick form pushes us away from seriousness and into irony. This might have something to do with the limerick's anapestic meter, which is so far removed from the natural cadences of English that it almost always sounds strange and a little bit transgressive. And because anapestic phrases occur so rarely in standard English, limericks often require inverted word orders, sloppy end rhymes, non-standard constructions, and other usage choices that detract from the seriousness of a poetic venture.

More importantly, though, we have heard funny limericks (many of them obscene) all of our lives, and most of us will die without ever hearing a serious one. The form itself comes with all kinds of social and cultural assumptions that we just can't slip on and off when it suits us, and these assumptions are part of the implied understanding between the writer and the reader. If somebody did write a completely unironic limerick, it would be so incompatible with its own form that it would violate our expectations and become, therefore, ironic.

---

9. Just for the record, some ravens have been taught to say "Nevermore." See http://www.youtube.com/watch?v=rIX_6TBeph0 (accessed April 28, 2014).

This is true of a lot of poetic forms. The seventeen syllables of a haiku emphasize the ephemeral nature of experience. You will probably never read a serious haiku about eternity. The classical ode, which evolved from the oppositional movements of Greek choruses, is designed to consider a proposition from multiple perspectives. Sonnets are almost always about love. The forms themselves create expectations. And when poets choose to write in these forms, those expectations become part of what their poems mean.

Sometimes, works of literature will shift from one form to another. When this happens, we should pay very close attention, because shifts in form always mean something. If a poem starts out with 500 lines of perfect iambic pentameter couplets, and then all of a sudden shifts to free verse, we need to figure out why. If we are reading a realistic novel and discover that three of the middle chapters consisting entirely of knock-knock jokes, we can assume that the author wants to communicate something about those three chapters. Major formal shifts in literary works are always worthy of attention.

One of the most dramatic formal shifts in all of world literature occurs between the second and third chapters of the Book of Job. The first two chapters are something like a children's bedtime story. These prose chapters are primarily narrative, plot-driven, and constructed in the third person. Then, suddenly, everything changes. The third-person prose becomes first-person poetry, the plot-driven tale becomes metaphor-driven introspection, and the simple and understandable language becomes excruciatingly complex. Unless we choose to believe that the author of the book was incompetent or insane, we must try to figure out what this major formal shift means—for we can be absolutely certain that it means something.

Literature creates truth in collaboration with readers

The first paper I wrote as an English major in college was truly awful. The paper was on *Beowulf*, and my argument went something like this: Beowulf was a king and therefore a member of the upper class. Everybody thought that Grendel was a monster, but, really, he just wanted to get a drink at the tavern where all of the rich guys hung out. He was a member of the oppressed proletariat, and Beowulf was a symbol of the oppressive bourgeoisie. The whole poem is nothing less than the world's first great Marxist allegory.

Somehow, I managed to pass the class anyway—probably because the professor didn't want me back ever again. But when he gave me a low (but higher than I deserved) grade on the paper, I protested: Who are you to say that my interpretation of a poem is wrong? A poem means whatever I

say it means—why do you get to control the meaning of the text? When
I became a professor myself, I discovered that a shockingly large number
of English majors go through this phase. When young people first realize
that a work of literature can mean more than one thing, they immediately
leap to the conclusion that it can mean anything at all—that any imaginable reading is just as good as any other.

Going through this phase is an important part of developing a critical
mind, but so is growing out of it. All literary texts can support a limited
range of interpretations. The range can be very narrow, but never so narrow that it removes all possible interpretations but one. The range can
also be very broad, but never so broad that it permits any interpretation
whatsoever. Poems are not inkblots. They mean things. But they draw
their meaning from both the intentions of the author and the experiences
of the reader. This means that the range of possible interpretations must
account for the perspectives and life experiences of both.

Take, for example, the famous, but extremely confusing last two lines
of John Keats's "Ode on a Grecian Urn":

> "Beauty is truth, truth beauty,—that is all
> Ye know on earth, and all ye need to know."

It is pretty much anyone's guess what this means. Nobody knows for
sure. Or, rather, a lot of people know for sure, but they do not know for
sure in the same ways. Some interpreters read it as an anticipation of the
late nineteenth-century aestheticism of Oscar Wilde and Walter Pater—
something like, "Nothing in the world is inherently true or meaningful, so
the only truth we have access to lies in subjective aesthetic experience." Or
it might mean something more like, "So great is the power of truth that
anything true is also necessarily beautiful." This would align Keats with
the Platonists and Neo-Platonists who came before him. Or it could be an
ironic joke: "Get a life, dude, and stop talking to pottery!"

And it gets worse. We have multiple drafts of the original poem that
punctuate these lines differently. Some versions enclose the entire last two
lines in quotation marks—"Beauty is truth, truth beauty, / That is all you
know in life and all you need to know"—thereby attributing the entire sentence to the urn. Other versions include only the words "Beauty is truth,
truth beauty" in quotation marks, which means that the rest of the sentence
could be read as the narrator's response to the urn ("that is all you need to
know, you stupid, old vase") or the narrator's or the poet's closing advice to
the reader (Keats's use of the plural "ye" would tend to support this reading).

During the first half of the twentieth century, most of the towering figures of the New Criticism —T. S. Eliot, Cleanth Brooks, M. H. Abrams, Douglas Bush, Hugh Kenner, and Walter Jackson Bate to name just a few—offered their own reading of these two perplexing lines of poetry.[10] They came up with some wonderfully insightful readings, proving that the same poem could mean many things to many people. But they also showed how the facts of the text constrain its interpretation. "Ode on a Grecian Urn" cannot mean anything at all. It is not about baseball, or trains. And (a thousand or so term papers aside) it is most certainly not an allegory of the way that the bourgeoisie oppresses the proletariat.

Literature can support contradictory readings that are both true

A favorite trick of great writers is to take a story that we think we know and shift our experience of it by telling it from a different point of view. The popular Broadway musical *Wicked,* based on a novel by Gregory Maguire, does this with the Wicked Witch of the West from the *Wizard of Oz.* By a giving name and a set of motivations to a character formerly portrayed as simply evil, *Wicked* forces us to reconsider our previous experience with the story and to reevaluate what we mean when we call someone wicked.

Two and a half millennia ago, around the time that Job was written, a spectacularly talented writer named Euripides did the same thing for Medea, one of the great villains of the ancient world. Everybody in Euripides's audience knew that Medea had killed her own children to punish her husband, Jason, for deserting her. But when a great poet gave her words of her own, he allowed her to express her anguish at Jason's betrayal and become a human being instead of a caricature. However, unlike Elphaba in *Wicked,* Medea does not become a heroine. The new perspective does not erase or excuse the horror of her evil deed; it merely complicates our ability to see her in only one way.

I have found that students struggle with *Medea* more than any other text that I teach regularly—not because it is hard to understand, which it isn't, but because they cannot arrive at a stable interpretation of their own feelings about its main character. On the one hand, they feel sympathy for Medea, whom Jason treats horribly. After convincing Medea to kill her own brother to save his life, he casts her aside like an empty sack so he

---

10. A good sampling of the critical debate over the ending of "Ode on a Grecian Urn," including essays by Bate, Bush, Abrams, has been anthologized by Jack Stillinger in *Twentieth Century Interpretations of Keats's Odes: A Collection of Critical Essays.*

can marry the daughter of a king. His self-justifying speeches expose the extreme limits of just how big of a jerk a human male can be.

When Jason tells Medea that nothing she has ever done for him matters because Aphrodite made her fall in love with him (and thus deserves all of his gratitude), my female students often start hitting any male in the vicinity just on principle. But then they suddenly realize that Medea kills her own children because she recognizes, correctly, that she cannot complete her revenge on Jason while their children are still live. At this point, students often experience an almost unmanageable cognitive dissonance between wanting to see Jason suffer and being horrified at how Medea makes him suffer. This conflicted response shows that Euripides could bring his audience to two mutually exclusive conclusions at the same time (that Jason was properly punished and that Jason was improperly punished) without providing an easy way to reconcile the contradiction. Another way to say this is that Euripides was a great poet.

The Book of Job overwhelms us with similar contradictions: 1) Satan is both correct and incorrect about Job's motives in the frame tale, 2) the text both rejects and enshrines the principle of divine reward, and 3) God both answers and refuses to answer Job's questions when He speaks from the whirlwind. Different starting assumptions about these parts of the story (and many more) lead to different insights that will not always resolve themselves into a single, internally consistent reading of the poem.

And that's OK. Unlike historians, who must try to account for everything that happened in the past, or scientists, who must generate predictions that hold up under all testable circumstances, poets and their readers can live in ambiguity. Keats called this "Negative Capability," which he defined as "capable of being in uncertainties, mysteries, doubts, without any irritable reaching after fact and reason." Walt Whitman put it even better in his famous "Song of Myself": "Do I contradict myself? Very well then I contradict myself, / I am large, I contain multitudes."[11] Job, too, is large, and both the character and the poem contain multitudes.

Literature can be a powerful way to test philosophical propositions

Cognitive scientists have long been puzzled by the great importance that humans place on deliberate fictions. Why should a species whose survival depends on true information devote so many resources to the

---

11. John Keats, *The Complete Poems*, 344–45. Walt Whitman, "Song of Myself," lines 1324–26, in *The Works of Walt Whitman*, 84.

production and consumption of stories that everybody knows to be false? One of the few things that both cognitive psychologists and literary critics agree on is that fictional narratives give us the ability to frame debatable propositions in our minds in a way that allows us to evaluate them imaginatively before expending the resources to evaluate them concretely. In the beginning, proposition-testing "stories" were probably very simple, like "hunting at night would be dangerous." It would certainly be safer to tell a story about night hunting than to actually try it. Any good storyteller could come up with plenty of imaginary dangers to "prove" the danger of roaming around the savannah after dark.[12]

As human culture evolved, imaginative literature began to function more as a way to test a culture's most important propositions. One of the first known works of literature, *The Epic of Gilgamesh*, tests the ways that a great king responds to the inevitability of death and the desire to be remembered (building walls for his people = good; going into the forest to kill something big = bad). Aristophanes's outrageously funny play *Lysistrata*, written during the worst days of the Peloponnesian War, tests the intriguing hypothesis that the women of Athens and Sparta could do a better job managing the war effort than the men who started it.

During the Enlightenment, literary narratives became a major tool for testing the propositions of philosophers. Voltaire's *Candide*, for example, was constructed to test Leibniz's mathematical proposition that we live in the best of all possible worlds (see Chapter Nine). Cervantes's *Don Quixote* tests, among other things, the proposition that reading books prepares one for life. Swift's *Gulliver's Travels* is a four-part test of the Enlightenment definition of a human being as a "rational animal." Each of these propositions fails the test. Candide moves from tragedy to tragedy with no hint of God's goodness. Don Quixote reads thousands of books that leave him hopelessly ill prepared for the real world. And the only completely rational animals that Swift can come up with are talking horses. These literary works become elaborate thought experiments that subject a philosophical assertion to intense logical scrutiny.

The Book of Job is precisely this kind of literary work. It sets out to test a very clear, very common theological proposition: God rewards righteousness and punishes wickedness. For the test to work, the poet must control the variables. Job can't just be sort of OK; he must be the most

---

12. For a survey of the various theories about the adaptive advantages of fictional narratives, including proposition testing, see Michael Austin, *Useful Fictions: Evolution, Anxiety, and the Origins of Literature*, 4–12.

perfect and upright man who has ever lived. His suffering can't be just moderately bad; it must be the most gruesome torment ever visited upon a human being. This way, we can't be distracted with extraneous questions like, "Was Job really so good that we can't explain his suffering by some sin in his life somewhere?" or "Was his suffering really suffering, or was it just a blessing in disguise?" The poet places these questions out of bounds so that we cannot use them to sidestep the essential fact of the story: Job is innocent, yet he suffers.

The Value of Poetic Truth

At the end of the Job poem, before we slip back into the frame, God appears to Job in a whirlwind and asks him rhetorical questions for four complete chapters (38–41). If we read Job as a history book, we must then read these four chapters as the longest direct quotation from God in the entire Bible, which gives the text an almost unimaginable amount of authority to appeal to. Any time the god of an entire Universe speaks four chapters of excellent poetry to somebody we had better pay attention.

We lose the sheer weight of this authority when we conceive God's final speech as the words of a poet, no matter how great, imagining what God might say in a certain situation. I believe that this, for many people, is the primary objection to seeing Job as a work of imaginative literature. People find comfort in the certain knowledge that God spoke to Job. They do not want to give up this comfort, and they do not want to concede that any part of the Bible might not be historically true because they are afraid that they will not then be able to believe anything it says.

But we have nothing to be afraid of when we read a work like Job the way that it asks to be read. God can inspire poets, and when He does, the resulting scripture will be a poem—and will therefore be true the way that poems are true. We can read the literary parts of the Bible as literature, the historical parts as history, and the prophetic parts as prophecy without questioning the truth of any part. All we have to do is acknowledge that the Old Testament contains many different kinds of writing (a fact that should be obvious to anybody who reads it) and that different kinds of writing can be true in different ways. To read and understand the Hebrew Bible on its own terms, and to fulfill our sacred mandate to seek learning by study and also by faith (D&C 88:118), we must make an effort to understand what it means for a poem to be true.

Chapter Three

The Frame Tale
(1–2; 42:7–17)

And the original Archangel or possessor of the command of the heavenly host is called the Devil, or Satan, and his children are called Sin and Death. But in the book of Job, Milton's Messiah is called Satan.
—William Blake, *The Marriage of Heaven and Hell*

> *I never hated those who were like you:*
> *Of all the spirits that negate*
> *The knavish jester gives me least to do.*
> *For man's activity can easily abate,*
> *He soon prefers uninterrupted rest;*
> *To give him this companion hence seems best*
> *Who roils and must as Devil help create.*
> —"Prologue in Heaven,"
> Johann Wolfgang von Goethe's *Faust*

The Prologue in Heaven: Starring . . . Satan

"Imaginary evil is romantic and varied," writes Simone Weil in *Gravity and Grace*, while "imaginary good is boring."[1] Perhaps this explains why nearly every Western Literature class in the world teaches Dante's *Inferno*, while *Paradiso* can't even be found in mid-sized libraries. It could also explain why the devil in *Paradise Lost* has become one of the most recognizable literary characters in all the world's poetry, while even most English professors couldn't pick Milton's God out of a police lineup. And it is certainly why the character of Satan, who speaks in only six of Job's more than 1,000 verses, has become, in subsequent retellings of the story, the star of the show.

---

1. Simone Weil, *Gravity and Grace*, 62–63.

Satan's role in the Book of Job is minimal, but absolutely essential to everything that happens later. In the Prologue, God points to Job as a truly righteous man, and Satan responds that Job (and by implication all human beings) is only righteous because God pays him so well, an accusation that sets the entire plot of Job in motion. God allows Satan to take away everything that makes Job happy—his wealth, his children, and finally his good health. This sets up a controlled-variable experiment to determine if Job will still praise God in the absence of any reward for doing so. At stake in this experiment is the idea of righteousness itself, for, if Satan is correct, then we must conclude that there is no such thing—only enlightened self-interest masquerading as morality.

In literary terms, Job's Satan can be considered a "trickster"—a powerful force that introduces chaos into a story by disregarding conventions. Tricksters abound in the world's mythology and folklore: the African spider-god Anansi is a trickster, and so is the Native American spirit Coyote. Loki and Pan are the trickster-gods of Norse and Greek mythology respectively. Tricksters often bring about good things even though they rarely try to; and they always make stories more interesting. Their primary function in folk literature is to set complicated plots in motion by introducing elements of randomness into previously controlled environments, which is precisely what Satan does in the Book of Job.

Characters based on Job's Satan have major roles in most of the modern adaptations, including Archibald MacLeish's *J.B.*, Neil Simon's *God's Favorite*, and Elie Wiesel's *The Trial of God*. These works confine most of their action (albeit in very different ways) to the frame portion of Job—which lends itself to dramatic adaptation much better than the long, contemplative dialogues of the poem. And in all of these plays, the role of Satan eclipses the role of God, who gets a speaking part in only one of the three (*J.B.*). In the other two, the only information that we get about the God character comes from His Satanic counterpart.

In most modern adaptations of Job (and "modern" in this context means since the middle of the seventeenth century), the Satan figure must bear the stamp of the artist's uniqueness. God must always be perfect and godlike, while Job must always be miserable and put upon. But Satan can represent whatever qualities a story happens to need. For the Romantic poet William Blake, Satan is a necessary principle of energy and motion. For Neil Simon, he is a New York City schlemiel just trying to get Job to renounce God so he can punch out and go home. And for Elie Wiesel, he is both the defender of God and the source of anti-Semitic hatred.

The ideological plasticity of Satan, as much as our fascination with evil, contributes to the important role that he plays in the Job tradition—despite playing such a small part in the actual Book of Job. But even in the Job frame, Satan's small role has huge implications for the story. Modern readers, of course, must always grapple with the shock of seeing a being they have long considered the source of all evil bantering with God like a poker buddy. But even ancient readers must have been impressed by the ability of this being to set an epic plot in motion with just a few well-chosen sentences. When they amplify Satan's role far beyond the original text, modern dramatists are merely tapping the dramatic potential that has always been part of Satan's cameo appearance in the Job story.

By a wide margin, the literary adaptation of Job with the greatest cultural heft is also the one that expands Satan's role the most dramatically: Johann Wolfgang von Goethe's masterpiece, *Faust*.[2] Goethe, of course, is working primarily within a different folk-narrative context; by 1808, the Faust legend had been part of Germanic folk culture for centuries. But Goethe added a new twist. By beginning his story with a Job-inspired conversation between God and Satan (called "Mephistopheles" in the play), Goethe completely reimagines the Faust legend. Instead of being a story of damnation, as it had always been before, Goethe's *Faust* becomes a story of testing and redemption.

In Goethe's version of the prologue, the Lord points to Faust, as He once pointed to Job, as humanity's best hope to refute the Devil's cynical accusation that human beings are aimless and trivial. In the drama that follows, Mephistopheles leads God's favorite down an almost unimaginable path of sin and deprivation—much as he does in Christopher Marlowe's earlier play, *Doctor Faustus* (1589). But in Goethe's version, it is all part of God's plan to turn Faust into a great man. In the end, the hero will be redeemed—not in spite of Mephistopheles's interference, but because of it. As the Lord says of Faust in the Prologue:

> Though now he serves me but confusedly,
> I shall soon lead him where the vapor clears.
> The gardener knows, however small the tree,
> That bloom and fruit adorn its later years.[3]

---

2. The first part of *Faust* was published in 1808 and the second part in 1832. It is only by reading the two parts together that we can perceive the outlines of the Job story, as it is not until *Faust, Part II* that we can see the forward movement in the character Faust that God alludes to in the Prologue.

3. See "Prologue in Heaven" in *Faust*, trans. Walter Kaufman, 87.

God, in other words, is in charge of the whole shebang, and He needs the Devil to help Him prod Faust out of his complacent despair. Satan is an unwilling agent of God's benevolent will because he lacks God's foresight and ability to manipulate events. Even when he actively tries to frustrate God's plans, Satan does exactly what God wants him to do. Like the rest of us, he serves God because he cannot do otherwise. God is a chess master who has already figured out all the moves—though we mere readers have to get all the way to the end of *Faust Part II*, the sequel written nearly twenty-five years after *Part I*, to understand the endgame.

The story of a Chess-master God manipulating his adversary from a distance has become a standard Christian interpretation of the Book of Job—or, at least, of the frame portion of the book that so many people mistake for the whole. This metaphor becomes much more concrete in *The Undying Fire*, H. G. Wells's 1919 novelistic adaptation of the Book of Job. In the "Prologue in Heaven" portion of the novel, Wells presents the dialogue between God and Satan as a game of chess:

> The Ruler of the Universe creates the board, the pieces, and the rules; he makes all the moves; he may make as many moves as he likes whenever he likes; his antagonist, however, is permitted to introduce a slight inexplicable inaccuracy into each move, which necessitates further moves in correction. The Creator determines and conceals the aim of the game, and it is never clear whether the purpose of the adversary is to defeat or assist him in his unfathomable project.[4]

After the prologue, Wells recasts the entire Job story as the battle to save an experimental British school—combining his interest in theology with his passion for educational reform. The schoolmaster, Mr. Job Huss (pronounced "us" by the other characters) rallies to save the school after a series of disasters that claim the lives of several students. His main opponents are three members of the Board of Directors—Sir Eliphaz Burrows, Mr. William (Bill) Dad, and Mr. Joseph (Joe) Farr—who visit him when he contracts cancer and try to replace him as headmaster so they can dumb down the curriculum and evict the liberal arts. Other characters include Job's surgeon, Dr. Elihu Barrack, and his wife, both of whom accuse him of folly when he continues to believe in God and in the divinity of the human mind.

The debates between Job and his Comforters stick pretty close to the original script. The three directors chastise Job for not preventing the ca-

---

4. H. G. Wells, *The Undying Fire*, 3.

lamities in the school and argue that he is to blame for them. Job continues to proclaim his innocence after every encounter. In the climax, however, Wells introduces a radical (though not quite unprecedented) interpretive move: when Job goes under the knife and has a vision, the voice that asks, "Who is this that darkeneth counsel by words without knowledge?" belongs, not to God, as he initially believes, but to Satan. In much the same way that Goethe does, Wells lets God completely off the hook for all of the bad stuff that happens.

Both Goethe and Wells expand Satan's visibility in the Job story dramatically, while, at the same time, reducing Satan's influence on the plot. As the prologues make clear, they are both stories about God's master plan for the protagonists' benefit. In trying to frustrate God's plans, Satan becomes a necessary, if unwilling agent of their success. God tricks Satan into testing Job so that Job can pass the test and receive even greater rewards than he already had. This provides an easy answer to the question, "Why does Job suffer?" Job suffers because God knows that he must suffer in order to get more stuff. Everything that happens in the story flows from God's love and benevolence and works for Job's good.

When we bring this same narrative logic back to the original Book of Job, we turn the most profoundly disturbing book in the Bible into a happy affirmation of God's great plan for our happiness. All of the hard things in our lives that we struggle to understand are indeed part of a bafflingly complex divine strategy whose only objective is to make us happy. As LDS apostle Hugh B. Brown said in his famous talk "God Is the Gardener," not referring to Job but echoing Goethe's language in *Faust*: "Someday, when you are ripened in life, you're going to shout back across time and say, 'Thank you, Mr. Gardener, for cutting me down; for loving me enough to hurt me.'"[5]

The "Chess-Master Gardener God" theory may very well describe the way that God works. (I really hope that it does, in fact.) It is a very comforting way to read the Book of Job, and it is certainly within the range of interpretations that the text will support. However, it would not have been possible for anyone in the sixth century B.C. to read or understand Job in this way. It would have required understandings of God and Satan that simply did not exist at the time. The Yahweh (Jehovah) of the sixth century B.C. was nothing like the warm, fuzzy grandfather god we

---

5. Hugh B. Brown, "God Is the Gardener," May 31, 1968. Available at http://speeches.byu.edu/?act=viewitem&id=111 (accessed April 28, 2014).

know today.[6] He was harsh, vindictive, demanding, and often cruel. And the Satan of the Job frame is nothing like the diabolical majesty of the Christian tradition. In fact, the Satan of Job is not even "Satan" in the original text. He is *hasatan*, or "the satan"—an office rather than a proper name. To grasp how the author of Job uses the frame to set up the poem, we need to understand a little bit more about who the satan was and where he came from.

The Role of the Satan in the Celestial Court

Satan may well have come into the Hebrew Bible, and therefore into the Christian tradition, through this "accuser" figure in the Book of Job. He does not appear as a developed character anywhere else in the Old Testament—the Garden of Eden doesn't count, as it is the Christian tradition and not the Hebrew text itself that equates Satan with the serpent in Genesis. The Jews in sixth-century Babylon had no reason to suspect that Satan might have been the serpent who tempted Adam and Eve. In fact, the Jews in the sixth century B.C. were just starting to develop an understanding of a semi-divine, wholly evil counterpart to Yahweh—who had earlier represented both the good and the evil aspects of divinity.

As the prominent religious historian Jeffrey Burton Russell explains, human cultures have always attributed both ultimate good and ultimate evil to their gods. When the Hebrews moved to a complete monotheism, they attributed all of the aspects of "the gods," good and evil, to a single god. "Since Yahweh was the one god," Russell writes, "he was both light and darkness, both good and evil."[7] As Jewish culture became more concerned with ethical behavior, they separated out the negative aspects of

---

6. For more on the divine name Yahweh, see David Bokovoy, *Authoring the Old Testament: Genesis–Deuteronomy*, 2, 33.

7. Jeffrey Burton Russell, *The Devil: Perceptions of Evil from Antiquity to Primitive Christianity*, 177–78. Russell, a practicing Catholic, takes pains to point out the fact that the concept of Satan evolved does not mean that it is an illegitimate theological construct. "The fact that the Devil is not fully developed in the Old Testament," he writes, "is not a ground for rejecting his existence in modern Jewish and Christian theology. That would be the genetic fallacy: the notion that the truth of a word—or concept—is to be found in its earliest form. Rather, historical truth is development through time" (174). For an LDS perspective on the developing concept of Satan, see Charles R. Harrell, *"This Is My Doctrine": The Development of Mormon Theology*, 193–98.

Yahweh and attributed them to a figure of ultimate evil, leaving Yahweh free to take on a more benevolent aspect and become the loving Heavenly Father of Christian and later Jewish thought.

There was no better place in the ancient world to develop such a theology than the Persian Empire. The Persians were not quite monotheists, or believers in a single god; they were dualists. The Zoroastrian religion that they followed believed in two god-figures locked in an eternal struggle with each other. Ahura Mazda was the creator and source of all goodness and light; Ahriman was his enemy and the source of all darkness. As Russell explains, there is some evidence that Zoroastrian dualism influenced the evolution of Satan. "Ahriman and Satan show certain intrinsic similarities," he writes, and "these similarities become striking in Hebrew thought following the exile, when Hebrew writers could easily come into contact with Zoroastrian ideas in Babylonia."[8]

Though we can see glimpses of the devil we know in the Book of Job, the Satan of the frame narrative is nothing like the personification of evil that he would eventually become. He does not have a tail or cloven hoofs. Nor does he reside in the underworld or torment sinners after they die. "The satan" is a member of God's royal court like "the messenger" or "the advisor," known only by his function. And to understand the function of a satan, we need to look at the shape of the Persian court as it would have been seen by the Jews who remained in the Empire and created what Christians now call the Old Testament.

In his *Anchor Bible* commentary, Marvin Pope expresses the common opinion that a satan was a kind of intelligence agent—"a kind of spy roaming the earth and reporting to God on the evil he found therein." The name "satan" comes from the verb "to accuse," which would make sense for the kind of role that Pope suggests—a highly placed information-gatherer who would be "ready to accuse and indict his victim and serve as a prosecutor."[9] This is precisely the context of the only other occurrence of *hasatan* in the Old Testament, found in Zechariah 3:1, when the prophet Zechariah has a vision of Joshua "standing before the angel of the Lord and the accuser [*hasatan*] standing at his right to accuse him."

As in Job, the satan in Zechariah combines the functions of a district attorney and a star witness for the prosecution. His job is to keep the Kingdom of God safe by rooting out discontentment and sedition wherever it might be. This understanding of Satan is also supported by what we

---

8. Russell, *The Devil*, 218.
9. Marvin Pope, *The Anchor Bible: Job*, 10.

know of the workings of Persian Empire, which conquered Babylon and freed the Jews in 539 B.C. Glossing the contemporary historian Herodotus, Pope explains:

> the vast Persian Empire, as organized by the genius of Darius the Great, depended in great measure for its security on the well-developed system of highways and communications which linked the provincial capitals, and on an efficient intelligence agency which kept the powerful governors under surveillance to detect and prevent sedition and rebellion. Some of these inspectors or master spies were known as "The King's Eye" and "The King's Ear." "The Eye of the King" appears to have been an officer in constant attendance on the king.[10]

Given the strong likelihood that 1) the original Job frame tale came from a Persian or other Near Eastern source, and 2) the composition of the Job poem occurred after the Persians had conquered Babylon and freed the Jews, it is extremely likely that the author imagines the satan, who comes to the court of heaven after "roaming all over the earth" (Job 1:7), as something like a shadowy member of the great Persian secret police—a political spy with a charge to root out sedition and accuse disloyal officials before the king.

Because such a figure would have had the power to ruin anybody in the kingdom with an accusation, he would certainly have been feared, resented, and perceived in a sinister light. This sort of divine Gestapo agent is a plausible starting point for the gradual evolution of the Satan we know—a being of ultimate evil who tempts people to sin and then tortures them for eternity when they succumb to his temptations. But in Job, we are not yet there. The satan is not Satan; he is a functionary in the heavenly court who may have a bit of an attitude but who still takes his marching orders from God.

The Challenge

When we encounter the satan in the Book of Job, it is "one day when the divine beings presented themselves before the LORD" (1:6). When God asks for a report, the satan answers that he has been "ranging over the earth . . . from end to end" (1:7). God's next question assumes that the satan has been looking for something in particular—not for a dishonest person (what age has not had plenty of those?), but for an honest one—

---

10. Ibid., 10.

somebody who might reverse the cynical view of human nature that this servant of the Lord appears to have developed.

When God invites the satan to consider Job, He is responding—as only God can—to the unspoken accusation in the latter's report that human beings are selfish and corrupt. Ironically, this is the same accusation that Yahweh himself once made to Abraham, who convinced God to spare Sodom and Gomorrah for the sake of ten righteous men—but who, alas, could not find even one (Gen. 18:16–33). In Job, however, God has already found the right person to prove his point: "Have you noticed my servant Job?" He asks the satan. "There is no one like him on earth, a blameless and upright man who fears God and shuns evil!" (1:8). And this is where we see what was really on the satan's mind: "Does Job not have good reason to fear God? Why, it is You who have fenced him round, him and his household and all that he has. You have blessed his efforts so that his possessions spread out in the land. But lay Your hand upon all that he has and he will surely blaspheme You to Your face" (1:9–11).

This is a devastating question to those who have accepted the cheerful message of the frame narrative—and it is a question that too many readers have dismissed too lightly for too long. It accuses Job, and by extension all righteous people, of turning morality into a commercial transaction—something that we do primarily to get stuff. The first two verses of Job make this question inevitable. In verse one, we are told that Job "feared God and shunned evil." In the second verse, we are told that "seven sons and three daughters were born to him" and that "his possessions were seven thousand sheep, three thousand camels, five hundred yoke of oxen and five hundred she-asses." We can hardly fault the satan for thinking that Job's wealth might be God's reward for Job's righteousness. The text invites all readers to think the same.

Behind the satan's question lurks an assumption that works like corrosive acid on 2,500 years of human religious experience: the assumption that there is no moral value to actions undertaken primarily for gain. We may well do good things because somebody is paying us to do them, but this does not make us good people. Motivations matter, and self-interest—no matter how enlightened or forward looking—is at best a morally neutral survival instinct of the sort that makes a donkey follow a carrot. Selfishness never was righteousness.

Most religions would acknowledge the truth of this claim in the abstract, but this does not keep them from promising big rewards to those who behave in ways defined as "good." For the ancient Hebrews, who lacked a monetary economy and a well-developed concept of the afterlife, "rewards for righteousness" meant sons and she-donkeys. But Christians, who vastly expanded the afterlife to contain mansions of glory and streets paved with gold, can defer the promised reward until the hereafter. We can always imagine that we are being bribed by God—and whether the bribe consists of she-donkeys, blessings, or celestial glory, the underlying morality is the same.

When the satan brings this up in the divine court, God does not argue the underlying assumption. He does not say, "Well, of course I have rewarded Job for his righteousness, but that does not mean that he is not a good man," or "It is perfectly acceptable for people to expect me to reward them when they obey my commandments." Rather, He accepts the major premise (that obedience for the sake of reward has no moral value) and contests the minor (that Job only obeys God because he expects a reward). Also, God allows the satan to test this premise himself: "All that he has is in your power; only do not lay a hand on him" (1:12).

And, with these words, God signs the death warrant for Job's ten children and turns him into a pauper. Job is deprived of everything that once made him "wealthier than anyone in the East" (1:3). Modern interpreters have always been greatly bothered by the children. Losing camels and sheep is one thing, but how could God kill ten innocent children just to win a bet with an underling (and one that we now identify as the source of all evil). This would be, I believe, a nearly fatal objection to the story if one insisted on reading it as a historical record. I do not think I could be persuaded to believe in a God who would casually kill a man's whole family just to prove an abstract point to one of His minions.

When we read Job as a work of literature, however, the question shifts. We no longer have to ask the terrible question, "Why would a loving God do something like that?" We need only ask the much more palatable (and in many ways more interesting) question, "Why would a great poet create a scene in which God did something like that?" In all likelihood, the poet did not have much choice. An artist who adapts previous material is free to shape it around the edges but not to change the essential nature of the original. Cinderella has to have stepsisters, Superman always comes from Krypton, the *Titanic* must sink—the fundamental elements of the story have to remain in place or the adaptation just won't work.

Since the poet apparently wants to present the common story of Job faithfully in the prologue, and then dismantle its assumptions in the poem, Job's children must die. And Job responds to their deaths exactly as

Yahweh knew that he would: "Job did not sin, nor did he cast reproach on God" (1:22). Frame Job bears his misfortunes patiently, even cheerfully, declaring that one must worship the Lord in good times and in bad. He even has a little poem that he chants when things get rough:

> Naked came I out of my mother's womb,
> and naked shall I return there;
> the LORD has given, and the LORD has taken away;
> blessed be the name of the LORD. (1:21)

We should not ignore the irony of Frame Job expressing his cheerful complacency in verse in a section of the book otherwise dominated by prose. This doggerel poem becomes Job's first statement on his own suffering—a statement that is supplanted in every possible way by the much greater, much darker poem that follows. In the poem, there will be absolutely no discussion of either nudity or blessing the name of the Lord. But in the self-contained world of the frame, Job does not turn away from God when he loses his wealth and family, so the satan has to move on to Plan B.

Almost anybody could be compelled by sufficient physical pain to repudiate a deeply held belief. That is why torture works. This is the ace up the satan's sleeve when he walks back into the heavenly court after failing at his first attempt to get Job to curse God. The conversation goes much as before—a common feature of stories with roots in an oral tradition. The satan reports that he has been "roaming all over the earth" (2:2), and the Lord asks him if he has "noticed my servant Job"—and he adds, "He still keeps his integrity; so you have incited Me against him to destroy him for no good reason" (2: 3). This time, the satan responds with the certainty of one who still has his best card to play:

> Skin for skin—all that a man has he will give up for his life. But lay a hand on his bones and his flesh, and he will surely blaspheme You to Your face. (2:4–5)

The Lord assents, and, in the next verse we see Job afflicted with running sores all over his body, scratching himself with a broken pot.

The two phases of the satan's attack on Job function as rough allegories for the categories of religious incentive that we can call "promise of reward" and "fear of punishment"—both of which have always been part of religion's strategies for motivating desired behaviors. In Ancient Israel, this was pretty straightforward: if you were good, God gave you cattle and male children; if you were bad, you got stoned to death by your close friends and relatives. The promised rewards for virtue were always backed up by the threat of capital punishment for vice. This perhaps explains why "fear of God" is the closest that Ancient Hebrew can come to our word "religion."

Lots of people are still afraid of God today, and the Christian afterlife that allows rewards to be deferred to a glorious heaven also allows punishment to be deferred to an awful hell. Belief in a post-mortem pit of fire has declined a bit since the Middle Ages, but it remains a pervasive part of our culture. In a 2013 survey, forty-four percent of Americans reported that they believe in a hell that is "a place of suffering and punishment where people go after they die."[11] Job's culture did not have a concept of hell, but the picture of Job at the end of chapter 2—a man who has lost his livelihood and his ten children in rapid succession and now sits outside his tent scraping his running sores with a potshard—is as close to absolute misery as an Ancient Hebrew writer could come. And yet Job was a righteous man.

So, Who Won the Bet?

The satan disappears from the Book of Job after chapter 2, never to be seen or heard from again. When the frame resumes in chapter 42, Job acknowledges God's grandeur, and, in return, God blesses him with just as many children and twice as much wealth as he had before—a fairy-tale ending completely consistent with the fairy-tale nature of the Job frame. No mention is made of the opening drama between God and the satan, though most readers assume that God won the bet because, as long as we discount the 39 chapters of poetry between the beginning and the end, Job remains faithful to the Lord.

But the moment that God rewards Job for not cursing Him, He validates the satan's worldview and hands His adversary the victory. This, I believe, is the strongest argument for reading the final scene ironically. If we read it as the author's belief in virtue's ultimate reward, then we have to agree that the satan was right all along about both human and divine

11. "Majority of Americans Surveyed Believe Heaven and Hell Exist, the Devil and Angels Are Real and God Is Not Responsible for Recent U.S. Tragedies," *PR Newswire*, May 29, 2013,http://www.prnewswire.com/news-releases/majority-of-americans-surveyed-believe-heaven-and-hell-exist-the-devil-and-angels-are-real-and-god-is-not-responsible-for-recent-us-tragedies-209383941.html (accessed May 21, 2014). See also Susan Jones, "Poll: Americans' Belief in God Is Strong—But Declining," CNSNews, December 17, 2013, http://www.cnsnews.com/news/article/susan-jones/poll-americans-belief-god-strong-declining (accessed May 21, 2014).

nature. Far from being the exception to this rule, Job becomes the poster child. He endures more suffering than anyone else; therefore, he shows more faith in God—who then rewards him with twice as much stuff as he had back when he was merely the greatest man in the East. The message of Job to future generations becomes, "God will reward you for your righteousness eventually, so don't worry if He doesn't do so immediately."

If we read Job as some people do—as a Prologue, a Poem, and an Epilogue—we have no choice but to see it as the story of a great trial followed by an even greater reward. But this means admitting that the satan was right all along. We can eliminate this problem, though, by considering the entire frame (prologue and epilogue) as one version of the Job story and then reading the poem as an ironic commentary on that version. This makes the ending, like the beginning, part of what the poem critiques.

To see how this might work, think back to the Cinderella example in Chapter Two. In that story, the beginning and the end come from the traditional Disney version of *Cinderella*, while the feminist poem in the middle constitutes an uncompromising critique of the Disney ideology. After we have experienced the critique, we can't take the happy ending seriously—or at least not entirely seriously. When the poet, after having Cinderella critique princes and weddings and rich people for 10,000 lines, suddenly portrays Cinderella marrying the rich prince, we can be pretty sure that we are supposed to read at least some irony into her "happiness."

The ending to Job works the same way. The 10,000-word poem is a blistering critique of the assertion—which the frame associates with the satan—that people are rewarded or punished in life according to the morality of their actions. This is not an incidental part of the poem; it is the main point. When the poet returns us to the frame, I believe, he knows that we can't read the happy ending the way that his culture always had. He has given us no choice but to read this as an ironic poem's final irony—at least not if we think that the satan should lose the bet.

The adversary's challenge to God frames the Book of Job as a contest between two views of human nature. In the satan's view, human beings are Skinnerian machines—put in a stimulus and out pops a response. Latter-day Saints may well hear echoes here of the Satan we encounter in the Book of Moses—the pre-existent Lucifer who presented a plan to save all of God's children by forcing them to be righteous while on earth. When this plan was rejected, Mormons believe, Satan and a third of the host of heaven rebelled against God and "sought to destroy the agency of man" (Moses 4:3). In both Moses and Job, the adversary's greatest flaw is his failure of imagination: he cannot conceive of human beings who exercise meaningful moral agency.

On the other hand, the God of the Book of Job, like the God of the Book of Moses believes in the possibility of agency. He believes (and holds Job up as an example) that people are always able to choose, if not their circumstances, at least their responses to their circumstances. This is precisely the definition, of "spiritual freedom" that Holocaust survivor, Victor Frankel, proposes in *Man's Search for Meaning*:

> We who lived in concentration camps can remember the men who walked through the huts comforting others, giving away their last piece of bread. They may have been few in number, but they offer sufficient proof that everything can be taken from a man but one thing: the last of the human freedoms—to choose one's attitude in any given set of circumstances, to choose one's own way.[12]

In their own ways, both Frame Job and Poem Job exhibit this "last of human freedoms"—the former by refusing to succumb to despair, and the latter by refusing to bow to conventional wisdom. Too many people miss this. Those who read the beginning and the end and a few proof-texts in the middle almost always come away thinking that God rewards His followers in the end. When we find ourselves suffering adversity, no matter how great, we just need to bear it the way that Job did—and some day (in this life or the next), the accounts will all be balanced, and we will collect our great reward. Those who come to such a conclusion are (as Blake once said of Milton) of the devil's party without knowing it.

The Job frame challenges us to make the satan wrong, as Job made him wrong, by resisting the great temptation to tie moral behavior to incentive structures. This can be more difficult than it seems, as a vast portion of modern religious culture works hard to keep these ties in place, and human nature itself conspires in the enterprise. Human beings appear to have innate cognitive balancing mechanisms, tracing far back into the evolutionary past, that say, "if I do stuff, I should get stuff." Of course, so do gerbils—with the crucial difference that a gerbil cannot be persuaded to wait until after he dies for a pellet of food. The first story of Job that we encounter—the frame narrative that had circulated around the Ancient Near East for centuries—does little to portray human beings as free moral agents. For that, we must wait for the poem.

---

12. Victor Frankel, *Man's Search for Meaning* 75.

Chapter Four

The Wisdom Dialogue (3–27)

Human beings are meaning-makers, constantly trying to understand our world in terms of cause and effect. We desperately want to believe that the world makes sense, that it is a place where things don't just happen, they happen for a reason. . . . An unpredictable world, a world of randomness unregulated by cause and effect, would leave us uncomfortable.

—Rabbi Harold Kushner, *The Book of Job: When Bad Things Happened to a Good Person*

Patience, Schmatience

Imagine that you are watching an old, silent, black-and-white movie with no soundtrack. The film is grainy and inconsistent, the characters are barely developed, the acting is abysmal, and you can only discern a few basic elements of the story. Then, about ten minutes into the movie, everything changes into a high-end IMAX production with high-resolution color video and digital surround sound. Accompanying the technical change, the acting suddenly gets good and the characters become interesting. Though you can see that a few of the actors look a little bit like the ones in the old black-and-white movie, and the characters appear to have the same names, you know that you are watching a completely different movie. This is the sort of transition that we are supposed to experience between the second and the third chapters of the Book of Job.

The Job frame employs intentionally archaic language to tell an old story very simply. Its main character, Job, is flat and predictable. When he loses his children and all of his property, he just shrugs his shoulders and offers up a little bit of tepid doggerel verse. Frame Job is indifferent to his own suffering. He completely trusts God's justice—even in the matter of whether his own children will live or die. He never once asks why he suffers. He never complains. He never expresses even a faint desire that his situation might be different than it is. When his wife urges him to "blaspheme God and die," all he can say is, "Should we accept only good from God and not accept evil" (2:9–10)?

And then we switch to the IMAX version. Everything changes in chapter 3: the weak prose becomes strong poetry, the flat characters all become well-rounded and interesting, and Job, who was just singing ditties about being naked and happy, spends the entire chapter cursing his very existence:

> Perish the day on which I was born,
> And the night it was announced,
> "A male has been conceived!"
> May that day be darkness;
> May God above have no concern for it;
> May light not shine on it;
> May darkness and deep gloom reclaim it;
> May a pall lie over it;
> May what blackens the day terrify it.
> May obscurity carry off that night;
> May it not be counted among the days of the year;
> May it not appear in any of its months
>   . . .
> Why did I not die at birth,
> Expire as I came forth from the womb?
> Why were there knees to receive me,
> Or breasts for me to suck?
> For now would I be lying in repose, asleep and at rest.
>   (3:3–6; 11–13)

The parallel structures in these lines all work to intensify Job's suffering. This is an important element of Hebrew poetry that comes through in good translations. As the poem progresses, each verse tries to outdo the previous one in cursing various aspects of Job's conception and birth. The amplification goes on so long that it threatens to turn into a sort of grotesque gallows humor ("Yeah, and curse the bad rerun of M*A*S*H* that made my parents go to bed early that night"). But we know that Job has just lost ten children and all of his possessions and been stricken with sores all over his body. We know that, as he speaks these words, he is sitting outside and scraping himself with a jagged shard of pottery. We know we have nothing to laugh about.

Job 3 is the first part of the extended dialogue between Job and his three friends—Eliphaz, Bildad, and Zophar—who have travelled from their homes to comfort him. According to the frame, they have been sitting silently for seven full days, just commiserating with their companion. But when he begins to speak, they feel compelled to answer, and this sets up three rounds of speeches—seventeen in all—in which Job debates his Comforters about his own innocence and the meaning of his suffering. Eliphaz and Bildad speak three times each in this portion of the poem, Zophar speaks twice, and Job speaks a total of nine times. In each speech, Job addresses both his Comforters and God, and he demands to know the reason that he has been made to suffer.

The speeches in Job 3–27 make up what some scholars have called a "Wisdom dialogue"—a popular dramatic form in the ancient Near East. A Wisdom dialogue differs from a Socratic dialogue by allowing each participant's view a full hearing rather than leading inexorably to the truth of one position. "The ancient Near Eastern Wisdom dialogues seek neither to demonstrate the triumph of one voice over another nor to argue their way to a resolution," writes Carol A. Newsom in her masterful treatise *The Book of Job: A Contest of Moral Imaginations*. She continues, "Even in Job, the traditionalist voice is not a mere setup for the triumph of skepticism."[1] Everybody in a Wisdom dialogue has some part to play in defining the question and contributing to our final understanding of the debate.

Newsom's reading requires us to give a little bit more credence to the Comforters' arguments, and a little less credence to Job's concerns, than readers typically do. It requires us to see the Comforters, not as a single hive mind, but as three separate voices with three different points of view. It also requires us to realize that not everything they say is wrong, just as not everything Job says is right. All four participants in the Wisdom dialogue—Job and his Comforters—are groping toward truths and perspectives that none of them really has the ability to understand. As readers, we must approach all four perspectives as partial and incomplete. Wisdom dialogues occur among those searching for wisdom, not among those who have already found it.

Eliphaz Leads with Sunday-School Answers

The first Comforter, Eliphaz, takes his role very seriously. He does not (at least initially) suggest that Job suffers because he has sinned. Rather, he says everything that he can to try to make Job feel better. But his suggestions fall flat. They sound a lot like the kinds of suggestions we might today

---

1. Carol A. Newsom, *The Book of Job: A Contest of Moral Imaginations*, 85.

call "Sunday-school answers": pray, read the scriptures, follow the prophet, etc. These are the sorts of answers that one might give about a theoretical person's suffering ("Yes, Mr. Brown, I know you have had a bad day with all of your children dying and all, but try to remember that your Father in Heaven loves you"). These answers do not respond in any significant way to Job's real suffering. But how could they? The poet has designed Job's suffering to exceed what our existing narratives can explain. We should not be too hard on Eliphaz, therefore; the poet has set him up to fail.

But his failure can instruct us how not to treat a suffering friend. Nearly everything he says fits comfortably into the range of things that we might be tempted to say to a loved one who is enduring extreme pain or profound loss. These are not bad things to say. Eliphaz does not treat Job cruelly or even unsympathetically in this first speech. He simply insists on speaking when there is nothing he can say. Before we ever follow his example, we should consider how each of his suggestions sounds to the suffering Job.

1. Follow Your Own Advice

Eliphaz begins by reminding Job how he once himself comforted people in their suffering—subtly inviting Job to take the advice that he once dispensed:

> See, you have encouraged many;
> You have strengthened failing hands.
> Your words have kept him who stumbled from falling;
> You have braced knees that gave way.
> (4:3–4)

These remarks contain a touch of accusation—suggesting that Job can dish out advice better than he can take it. But they can also be read as a plea for help from an inexperienced Comforter to an experienced one, something like "I can't possibly put myself in your shoes, but you can put yourself in mine. Imagine that you were talking to somebody suffering as you now are. What would you say? Help me out here, because you are the master."

2. Trust God

Eliphaz's next point is often read as part of the Comforters' collective argument that Job must have sinned because suffering is itself a sign of God's displeasure. He does indeed seem to suggest such a thing in verse 7 ("what innocent man ever perished?"), but, in context, Eliphaz is saying something very different and much less critical of Job:

> Is not your piety your confidence,
> Your integrity your hope?
> Think now, what innocent man ever perished?
> Where have the upright been destroyed?
> (4:6–7)

Instead of suggesting that he has sinned, Eliphaz reminds Job that he is a righteous man who has lived a blameless life. God will ultimately make sure that Job is rewarded for his piety, and whatever he may be going through right now will end up being part of the great reward—so he should stop complaining and realize that God has something wonderful in store for him. This, we should recall, is precisely the point of the frame tale.

3. Nobody's Perfect

In verses 12 through 16, Eliphaz describes a vision that he had in the night. When everybody else was asleep, he was gripped with a sudden terror "causing all [his] bones to quake with fright"(4:14). An apparition appeared before him and said,

> Can mortals be acquitted by God?
> Can man be cleared by his Maker?
> If He cannot trust His own servants,
> And casts reproach on His angels,
> How much less those who dwell in houses of clay,
> Whose origin is dust,
> Who are crushed like the moth.
> (4:17–19)

The dramatic nature of this revelation contrasts with the banal nature of its content. Nobody can be righteous compared to God because, well, nobody is perfect. One suspects that Eliphaz felt the need to dress this up as a terrifying vision to mask its ordinariness and to make Job feel that this message comes directly from God.

But this raises the question of why Eliphaz would make this point to Job in the first place—especially after just saying that he was a pious man who has lived a blameless life. This is where he first drops the hint that Job might have done something to anger God—something that he should repent of. Under Eliphaz's logic, Job could not help but do something to offend God, since no human being can possibly be blameless in the eyes of the Almighty. So Job's task is now a simple one: he just has to figure out what it is that he has done wrong and ask God to forgive him.

4. Keep Calm and Carry On

In the beginning of chapter 5, Eliphaz criticizes Job for a specific behavior for the first time, responding to the anger against God that he displayed in his previous speech. Eliphaz warns Job that he shouldn't get so mad because his anger will have serious negative consequences:

> Vexation kills the fool;
> Passion slays the simpleton.
> I myself saw a fool who had struck roots;
> Impulsively, I cursed his home:
> May his children be far from success;
> May they be oppressed in the gate with none to deliver them;
> May the hungry devour his harvest,
> Carrying it off in baskets;
> May the thirsty swallow their wealth.
> (5:2–5)

The irony in these lines is almost unbearable. Nearly everything that Eliphaz points to as the possible result of misdirected anger has already happened to Job. His home has been ruined. His children have been cut off from help. And his rich possessions have already been snatched from him. This is why he is so angry. That Eliphaz fails to see the irony in his own remarks suggests that he still sees Job's suffering abstractly enough to recite from a script—"things to say when somebody is suffering." He does not know how to engage with Job as a real, suffering human being.

5. It Happens to Everyone

No sufferer wants to hear that their pain is not special, or that lots of other people are suffering too. Not only does this do nothing to ease our own pain, it robs us of the solace (such as it is) of thinking ourselves especially put upon and therefore unique. When somebody tells a person in pain that lots of other people feel the same way, they are really saying, "Don't be such a baby—lots of other people get through this without whining." And yet, this is one of the most common things that people say to their friends who have endured great pain or great loss. Eliphaz is no exception:

> Evil does not grow out of the soil,
> Nor does mischief spring from the ground;

> For man is born to [do] mischief,
> Just as sparks fly upward.
> (5:6–7)

Ironically, Job himself has long functioned as the ultimate sufferer against whom everybody else's suffering must fall short. People frequently compare their own or other people's trials to those of Job as a way of saying, "it could always be worse, so suck it up." Job, I suspect, would not be amused.

6. Pray

No Sunday school class could possibly get all the way to the end without an exhortation to pray. And no list of Sunday school answers would be complete without this generic response:

> But I would resort to God;
> I would lay my case before God,
> Who performs great deeds which cannot be fathomed,
> Wondrous things without number.
> (5:8–9)

This answer contains the same sort of irony that we have already seen in Eliphaz's exhortations: Job's first speech is primarily a prayer, or at least an appeal in which he lays his case before God. He will continue to make such appeals throughout the poem.

7. God Is Testing You Because He Loves You So Much

Eliphaz has already told Job that everybody suffers so he is nothing special, but he has apparently reserved the right to change his mind. For near the end of his speech, Eliphaz suggests that those who suffer—or at least those who suffer at the hand of the Lord—are special indeed because they are the ones that God loves most.

> See how happy is the man whom God reproves;
> Do not reject the discipline of the Almighty.
> (5:17)

Eliphaz's logic here appears to be somewhere between "there's no such thing as bad publicity" and "this hurts God more than it hurts you." By paying attention to Job, and caring enough to discipline him, God actually shows how much He cares.

8. *It's All Going to Be OK*

We should always remember that Eliphaz, like Job's other Comforters, really is a friend, and he is trying to do his best in an extremely difficult situation. He ends his speech the way that almost all of us would end it: with a resounding affirmation that things are going to work out in the end—and a tender description of how things will be when all of the unpleasantness is over:

> You will laugh at violence and starvation,
> And have no fear of wild beasts.
> For you will have a pact with the rocks in the field,
> And the beasts of the field will be your allies.
> You will know that all is well in your tent;
> When you visit your wife you will never fail.
> You will see that your offspring are many,
> Your descendants like the grass of the earth.
> You will come to the grave in ripe old age,
> As shocks of grain are taken away in their season.
> See, we have inquired into this and it is so;
> Hear it and accept it.
> (5:22–27)

Eliphaz's final words in chapter 5 are beautiful. They describe a utopian end for Job in which God becomes his personal caretaker. In this vision, Job has been healed from his physical ills. His property and his family have been restored to him, and he has many descendants. And he lives a long and prosperous life before finally "com[ing] to the grave in ripe old age." This is, in fact, precisely how the frame tale ends—and, therefore, how the poet's original audience knew that things would eventually turn out.

However, Job's answer to Eliphaz, found in chapters 6 and 7, shows that he has not been even slightly comforted by anything that his friend has said. He begins by repeating his wish that God would simply end his life, and then he scoffs at the idea that he should wait for the rewards that God has in store. Patience in the face of extreme suffering, Job asserts, is neither rational nor possible for mere human beings made of flesh. "What strength have I, that I should endure?" he asks ironically. "Is my strength the strength of rock? / Is my flesh bronze? / Truly, I cannot help myself; / I have been deprived of resourcefulness" (6:11–13).

Here we see another clear instance of the poet intentionally subverting the frame tale. According to the frame's ideology, the knowledge of an eventual reward should make Job perfectly content to endure his present suffering. Indeed, the whole point of the frame tale is to convince people to suffer all things happily so that they, like Job, can get great rewards in the end. But when Eliphaz makes precisely this point to Job—and suggests that he should stop complaining because God has great blessings in store for him, his advice falls flat.

But nothing in Eliphaz's first speech justifies Job's barbed response back to him:

> My comrades are fickle, like a wadi,
> Like a bed on which streams once ran.
> They are dark with ice;
> Snow obscures them;
> But when they thaw, they vanish;
> In the heat, they disappear where they are.
> Their course twists and turns;
> They run into the desert and perish.
> (6:15–18)

It is true, of course, that Job has suffered almost unthinkable deprivations and that Eliphaz gives a shallow, condescending response. We can learn a lot from Eliphaz about how not to comfort people. Eliphaz speaks more out of a perceived need to say something at a time when just listening—and showing love—was probably his best response. But we can also learn a lot from Job about how not to receive clumsy-but-well-meaning sympathy from our friends. Later in the dialogue, the three Comforters will make the kinds of mean-spirited and judgmental comments that could warrant the kind of response Job gives. But they haven't made these statements yet. Eliphaz's first speech diligently avoids the sentiments that Job's response presumes, and Job's biting response puts all three of his friends on the defensive for the rest of the dialogue. The breakdown of friendship between Job and the Comforters cannot all be laid at the feet of Eliphaz, Bildad, and Zophar.

And, really, Job is not mad at Eliphaz; he is mad at God, as the rest of his reply makes clear. Eliphaz just happens to be around to absorb Job's anger. Job reserves his fiercest barbs throughout the dialogue for any suggestion that he is being unfair to the God who is being unfair to him. To Eliphaz's suggestion that he not risk offending God with his constant complaining, Job thunders:

> On my part, I will not speak with restraint;
> I will give voice to the anguish of my spirit;
> I will complain in the bitterness of my soul.
> Am I the sea or the Dragon,

That You have set a watch over me?
When I think, "My bed will comfort me,
My couch will share my sorrow,"
You frighten me with dreams,
And terrify me with visions,
Till I prefer strangulation,
Death, to my wasted frame.
I am sick of it.
I shall not live forever;
Let me be, for my days are a breath.
What is man, that You make much of him,
That You fix Your attention upon him?
You inspect him every morning,
Examine him every minute.
Will You not look away from me for a while,
Let me be, till I swallow my spittle?
If I have sinned, what have I done to You,
Watcher of men?
Why make of me Your target,
And a burden to myself?
Why do You not pardon my transgression
And forgive my iniquity?
For soon I shall lie down in the dust;
When You seek me, I shall be gone.
(7:11–21)

At this point, all readers of Job must realize that we are no longer dealing with the guy who said, "the Lord gives and the Lord takes away; blessed be the name of the Lord."

Zophar and Bildad Take Off the Gloves

Job's reaction to Eliphaz's advice dramatically changes the dynamic between him and his Comforters. Here again, we should look at things from the Comforters' perspective before rushing to judge them too quickly as false friends. They have all, at considerable expense to themselves, travelled some distance to be with their friend in his time of need. They have sat with him for seven full days without saying a word, just sharing his misery. And when one of them dared to speak—to try to offer some genuine words of comfort and counsel, Job became furious and cursed them all—coming perilously close to blasphemy in the process.

At this point, Bildad and Zophar have clearly had enough. In their minds, they have reached out to Job in kindness, and before either of them even says a word, Job criticizes them as false friends. From here on out, the dialogue from the perspective of the Comforters becomes less about understanding or consoling Job and more about defending themselves and proving to Job that he is responsible for his own suffering.

In his rebuttal to Job's complaint, Bildad picks up on what will now become the Comforter's main theme: Job is being punished because he has sinned and that, if he wants to stop being punished, he needs to stop sinning and repent. As we will see in Chapter 7, Bildad is invoking one of the central tenets of the ancient Hebrew religion: the "law of retribution," or the belief that God rewards or punishes every individual with their just deserts:

> Will God pervert the right?
> Will the Almighty pervert justice?
> If your sons sinned against Him,
> He dispatched them for their transgression.
> But if you seek God
> And supplicate the Almighty,
> If you are blameless and upright,
> He will protect you,
> And grant well-being to your righteous home.
> Though your beginning be small,
> In the end you will grow very great.
> (8:3–7)

Bildad introduces a new wrinkle into the argument by insisting— with no discernible evidence—that Job's sons were killed because they sinned against God. And he follows up with the logical corollary that Job is suffering because of his own sins. In doing so, of course, Bildad is simply repeating one of the major arguments of the entire Hebrew Bible—from the opening chapters of Genesis, which show a man and a woman disobeying God and being punished, all the way through the prophets of the Babylonian Exile, who lament that the Jews caused their own destruction by their chronic disregard for Yahweh's commandments.

When Job protests his innocence, insisting that he has done nothing to merit God's punishment, Zophar comes in and reprimands him even more strongly. Zophar's speech escalates the conflict past anything that can reasonably be considered comforting a sufferer. Eliphaz's first speech genuinely attempts to give Job good advice, and though Bildad rebukes him for his apparent blasphemy, he at least still ends with the prediction that God will "yet fill [Job's] mouth with laughter, and [his] lips with shouts of joy" (8:21). Zophar's speech, in contrast, is almost all rebuke:

> Your prattle may silence men;
> You may mock without being rebuked,
> And say, "My doctrine is pure,
> And I have been innocent in Your sight."
> But would that God might speak,
> And talk to you Himself.
> He would tell you the secrets of wisdom,
> For there are many sides to sagacity;
> And know that God has overlooked for you some of your iniquity
> (11:3–6)

This exchange brings us to the core of the argument between Job and the Comforters. Job knows that he is innocent as a matter of personal experience, and he is deeply offended that his best friends refuse to acknowledge this. His friends, however, cannot allow him to be innocent because their worldview does not contain a category for "innocent sufferer." This becomes the main theme of the Wisdom dialogue: the conflict between truth deduced from first principles (innocent people do not suffer) and truth generalized from observation (Job is innocent and yet he suffers). This same conflict between truth deduced and truth observed has been with us for a very long time: think Galileo and his telescope or Darwin and his Galápagos finches. Human beings have a difficult time modifying our first principles when they contradict our own lived experience. It is all but impossible to do so when somebody else's story is at stake.

Round and Round and Round We Go

By simply existing, Job challenges our cherished illusion that we live in a world that we can predict and control. Religion is one way that we indulge this illusion. Science, politics, and history are others. And in nearly every era, human beings have been willing to engage in stunningly irrational forms of magical and conspiratorial thinking to avoid having to accept the proposition that things happen for no apparent or controllable reason. Most of us would much rather think like Job's Comforters than spend our lives staring into the scary face of randomness and cosmic indifference.

Job, therefore, sits in one of the most dangerous rhetorical spaces that a human being can occupy. The mere fact of his existence contradicts the core beliefs of his interlocutors. They cannot accept the possibility of an innocent sufferer, so they must either dispute his suffering (which they can plainly see) or reject his claims of innocence. Nearly all of the arguments in the final two rounds of speeches attempt to do the latter. Eliphaz, who has the gentlest nature of all the Comforters, begins the second cycle of speeches by expanding on his earlier argument that Job cannot be innocent because nobody is innocent:

> What is man that he can be cleared of guilt,
> One born of woman, that he be in the right?
> He puts no trust in His holy ones;
> The heavens are not guiltless in His sight;
> What then of one loathsome and foul,
> Man, who drinks wrongdoing like water!
> (15:14–16)

Again, we should notice here that Eliphaz still goes out of his way to avoid accusing Job directly. He keeps his argument on the theoretical level, arguing only that Job takes part in the depravity general to all human beings. Bildad and Zophar come closer to direct accusations by speaking, generally, of the fate of the evil man—with the clear implication that Job fits in this category. In the third cycle, however, even Eliphaz accuses him directly. "Is it because of your piety that He arraigns you?" the first Comforter asks ironically. "You know that your wickedness is great, And that your iniquities have no limit." Eliphaz then goes on to accuse Job of specific sins that we, as readers, know perfectly well he has not committed:

> You exact pledges from your fellows without reason,
> And leave them naked, stripped of their clothes;
> You do not give the thirsty water to drink;
> You deny bread to the hungry
> The land belongs to the strong;
> The privileged occupy it.
> You have sent away widows empty-handed;
> The strength of the fatherless is broken.
> (22:6–9)

Job responds to these critiques with more or less equal parts of sarcasm and anger. He expresses his deep disappointment that his friends choose to confront, rather than comfort him. If he were in their place, he insists, "I would encourage you with words, / My moving lips would bring relief" (16:5). But of his so-called Comforters, he says, "Time and again you humiliate me, / And are not ashamed to abuse me" (19:3). And he asks them in anguish, "Why do you pursue me like God, / Maligning me insatiably?" (19:22). But, as always, Job reserves the bulk of his anger in the poem for God, whom, he reasons, must be either incompetent or unjust—incompetent because He does not realize that Job is innocent or unjust because He does not care.

In Job's speeches, the book takes on the shape of a legal proceeding with Job as the accused and God as the absent accuser. Job persists in the belief that, if he could just get a fair hearing, he could either convince God of his innocence or win a judgment:

> Would that I knew how to reach Him,
> How to get to His dwelling-place.
> I would set out my case before Him
> And fill my mouth with arguments.
> I would learn what answers He had for me
> And know how He would reply to me.
> Would He contend with me overbearingly?
> Surely He would not accuse me!
> There the upright would be cleared by Him,
> And I would escape forever from my judge.
> (23:3–7)

As the Wisdom dialogue progresses, it becomes more and more apparent that, while Job and his friends differ on the question of Job's innocence, they share the same core theological beliefs. Job believes in a God of Rewards and Punishments just as much as his friends do. He never argues for a more sophisticated view of morality divorced from carrots and whips. He just thinks that God got it wrong and that, if he could just get a few minutes alone with the Big Guy, he could get everything cleared up. Without such an opportunity, Job refers to God as one "who has deprived me of justice" (27:2)—a formulation that, if not blasphemous in this context, comes very close to the line.

Job, then, ties the great question of God's justice to the much smaller question of Job's happiness. As Alexander Pope would write 2,000 years later, Job cries, "If man's unhappy, God's unjust."[2] This perspective simply inverts that of his Comforters, who argue, in effect, that if Job is unhappy, it can only mean that Job is unjust. All of the participants in the dialogue unequivocally accept the premise that a just God would never allow an innocent man to suffer. For Job this means that God cannot be just; for his Comforters it means that Job cannot be innocent. Nobody ever questions the premise itself. But this is precisely the premise that we, as readers,

---

2. Alexander Pope, *Poetry and Prose of Alexander Pope*, 125.

must scrutinize. The poet leaves us no choice. We cannot side with the Comforters, for we know that Job is innocent. Nor can we side with Job, for we know that God has not accused Job of anything. We must therefore reject entirely the rewards-and-punishments paradigm that Job and his Comforters share. The poet wants us to conclude for ourselves that this is not the way that the universe works.

The Wisdom dialogue works hard to bring us to this conclusion, but it works very differently than the more familiar Socratic dialogues that we find in the works of Plato (and in college classrooms throughout the country). In the Socratic dialogue, the principal character (usually Socrates) knows the truth but feigns ignorance to lead his interlocutors to this truth through a series of well-designed, but ultimately rhetorical questions. In the Wisdom dialogue, none of the characters knows the truth. Each struggles with partial information, incorrect assumptions, and flawed reasoning. And at the end of the dialogue, they are no closer to wisdom than they were when it started. Neither Job nor his Comforters benefit much from the exercise.

We as readers, on the other hand, benefit tremendously. Everything that the participants get wrong leads us closer to the poet's vision of the truth. It has often been noted that the dialogue between Job and his Comforters does not give us any good answers to the question of why innocent people suffer. But it is not supposed to. Rather, it provides us with a virtual encyclopedia of wrong answers. It shows us nearly every way that the question can be misunderstood, begged, elided, oversimplified, and otherwise mangled. And these are precisely the things that we need to know if we are going to collaborate with the poet to produce better answers ourselves.

Chapter Five

Odds before the End (28–37)

The book of Job arguably has more puzzles than any other book of the Bible. It starts and ends in prose, but the speeches of Job, his friends, and God are in poetry. It has many hapax legomena—*words appearing nowhere but here—as well as passages of such great obscurity that interpreters have sometimes felt obliged to change letters to make any sense of them. . . . Nevertheless, this challenging text has remained unchanged for a very long time.*
—Mark Larrimore, *The Book of Job: A Biography*

A Job Miscellany

In my own analysis, I have divided Job into four sections and devoted one chapter of this volume to each. Three of these divisions represent more or less natural divisions within the text: the frame narrative (1–2; 42:7–17), the Wisdom dialogue (3–27), and Yahweh's thundering final speech (38–42:1–6) all make sense as separate units. The current chapter contains everything else—those parts of the Book of Job that don't fit neatly into any of the other sections and which happen to have been grouped together by some writer or redactor in between the Wisdom dialogue and the final answer.

In Job 28 through 37, we find three short selections that are as different from each other as they are from any other part of the text. Two of these selections were almost certainly added after the fact, quite possibly by editors who wanted to blunt some of the more subversive implications of the original poem. The third was just as certainly intended to be the last part of the original poem before God shows up for the grand finale. I group them together here only because they appear sequentially in the final version of the text. The three selections are as follows:

The Hymn to Wisdom (28): Chapter 28 of Job is a stand-alone poem often called the Hymn to Wisdom, which argues that human beings can never find wisdom themselves because only God is truly wise. True

wisdom for human beings means trusting and obeying God. Though
the poem is not attributed specifically to any of the previous speakers, it
comes in between two sections attributed to Job and therefore presents
itself as part of one continuous speech consisting of chapters 26 through
31. Textual scholars almost unanimously believe that the hymn is "an
editorial interpolation, perhaps with the aim of introducing a pious
view of wisdom into this book that is such a radical challenge to the
guiding assumptions of other books of Wisdom literature."[1]

Job's Final Speech (29–31): Job's final speech—in which he surveys
his past righteousness, explains his present situation, and declares his
innocence—was probably once the only thing between the Wisdom
dialogue and Yahweh's final answer. Job's peroration functions like the
closing statement of a trial. The Comforters do not respond to any
part of this statement, and it appears to be addressed more to God
than to them. Job concludes the speech by casting the entire dialogue
in legal rhetoric and demanding 1) that God allow him to call a witness on his behalf, and 2) that "Shaddai would reply to my wit, or my
accuser draw up a true bill" (31:35).

The Speeches of Elihu (32–37): At some point in Job's evolution,
somebody that we cannot identify, for reasons that we can only guess
at, decided that Job's Comforters were not sufficiently vigorous in
their defense of God. This person created a fourth interlocutor named
Elihu to give a direct and systematic presentation of the arguments
that emerged organically during the Wisdom dialogue. In six chapters, Elihu repeats many of the arguments that occur in the Wisdom
dialogue (chapters 3 through 27), but he manages to reframe them
significantly, moving them from attacks on Job for declaring his innocence to a defense of God, whose motives are not available to human
beings. In this way, Elihu creates a theological bridge between the
speeches of the major participants and the final speech of God.

Let me be very clear that I do not mean to disparage or discount
either the Wisdom hymn or the speeches of Elihu by noting the scholarly
consensus that they were late additions to the manuscript. Like all of the
books of the Bible, Job went through centuries of editing, copying, redacting, and compiling before achieving the canonical form that we know
today. But this final form has been the text of Job for two thousand years;

---

1. Robert Alter, *The Wisdom Books*, 114.

it is part of the text that millions of people have read, learned from, developed faith in, fought about, and died for. The canonical Book of Job, as it has existed at least since the time of Christ, deserves great respect.

However, when we ignore overwhelming evidence of editorial redaction, we often end up trying to impose artificial uniformity of the text—thus missing some of the most important things that the interpolated portions can actually tell us. I believe that we can and should acknowledge a remarkable degree of coherence in the text while still recognizing the secondary nature of a few of its passages. This is not because we find these passages less important or less worthy of study than the primary text but because we can understand them better if we read them as ancient commentary on, rather than integral parts of, the original Book of Job.

The Hymn to Wisdom

Job has long been classified—along with Proverbs, Ecclesiastes, and a handful of the Psalms—as "Wisdom literature." Found throughout the ancient Near East, Wisdom literature departs from the usual biblical modes (prophecy, history, etc.) and attempts to teach moral or practical truths directly to its readers. In the final chapter of this volume, we will examine the Book of Job as part of the Wisdom tradition. To understand Job 28, however, we need only know that poems about and hymns to wisdom were relatively common in the culture that produced the Hebrew Bible. Some of these found their way into the Psalms (1, 19, 119), two very famous ones ended up in the early chapters of Proverbs (8 and 9), and one of them, "The Hymn to Wisdom," was interpolated into the Book of Job by somebody who either saw or wanted to create a connection between it and the rest of the text.

On its own terms, the Hymn to Wisdom is a profound and pious poem that we can read profitably without any reference to the rest of the story. Robert Alter describes as "more like Proverbs than Job."[2] It has both the optimistic outlook and the epigrammatic clarity that we often associate with the Book of Proverbs. Structurally, however, the hymn resembles nothing so much as a classical ode, a form that developed in Greece about the same time as wisdom literature developed in the Near East.

Ancient Greek odes evolved from the choral movements in classical drama. The speeches of the chorus were structured in three distinct

2. Robert Alter, *The Art of Biblical Poetry*, 92.

stages—the *strophe*, the *antistrophe*, and the *epode*—which each corre-
sponded to the movement of the chorus across the stage. The lyrical odes
that evolved from this choral movement were called "Pindaric Odes" after
their inventor, the Greek poet Pindar. Pindaric odes also have a three-
part structure, with the first stanza normally advancing a proposition, the
second stanza somehow opposing that proposition, and the final stanza
reconciling the opposition and declaring the meaning of the ode. In this
way, the poem can explore seemingly contradictory ideas before reconciling them into something like an authorial assertion.

Either by sheer coincidence, or because Greek culture had penetrated
much of the Ancient World during the centuries of the Hebrew Bible's
construction, the Hymn to Wisdom in Job has a structure very similar
to that of a Pindaric Ode. The first eleven verses of the poem constitute
a single stanza that praises human ingenuity, especially the ability that
people have acquired to mine the earth for rare metals, jewels, and other
items of great beauty and value:

> There is a mine for silver,
> And a place where gold is refined.
> Iron is taken out of the earth,
> And copper smelted from rock.
> He sets bounds for darkness;
> To every limit man probes,
> To rocks in deepest darkness.
> They open up a shaft far from where men live,
> [In places] forgotten by wayfarers,
> Destitute of men, far removed.
> Earth, out of which food grows,
> Is changed below as if into fire.
> Its rocks are a source of sapphires;
> It contains gold dust too.
> No bird of prey knows the path to it;
> The falcon's eye has not gazed upon it.
> The proud beasts have not reached it;
> The lion has not crossed it.
> Man sets his hand against the flinty rock
> And overturns mountains by the roots.
> He carves out channels through rock;
> His eyes behold every precious thing.
> He dams up the sources of the streams
> So that hidden things may be brought to light.
> (28:1–11)

The second stanza, which also consists of eleven verses, contrasts the human ability to find worldly treasures with the inability to find spiritual treasures. The same humans who find gold and precious gems with such ease cannot find wisdom no matter how hard they look. Humans can no more find wisdom themselves than birds could extract silver from a deep mine. We lack the tools necessary to bring either one to the surface:

> But where can wisdom be found;
> Where is the source of understanding?
> No man can set a value on it;
> It cannot be found in the land of the living.
> The deep says, "It is not in me";
> The sea says, "I do not have it."
> It cannot be bartered for gold;
> Silver cannot be paid out as its price.
> The finest gold of Ophir cannot be weighed against it,
> Nor precious onyx, nor sapphire.
> Gold or glass cannot match its value,
> Nor vessels of fine gold be exchanged for it.
> Coral and crystal cannot be mentioned with it;
> A pouch of wisdom is better than rubies.
> Topaz from Nubia cannot match its value;
> Pure gold cannot be weighed against it.
> But whence does wisdom come?
> Where is the source of understanding?
> It is hidden from the eyes of all living,
> Concealed from the fowl of heaven.
> Abaddon and Death say,
> "We have only a report of it."
> (28:12–22)

This third and final section of the Hymn to Wisdom repeats a core message of Proverbs and other Wisdom literature: that only God is wise. True wisdom requires a perspective that can transcend time and space. Since only God can do this, only God can ever attain wisdom. The wisest thing that the rest of us can do is to trust God and follow his laws:

> God understands the way to it;
> He knows its source;
> For He sees to the ends of the earth,
> Observes all that is beneath the heavens.
> When He fixed the weight of the winds,
> Set the measure of the waters;
> When He made a rule for the rain

And a course for the thunderstorms,
Then He saw it and gauged it;
He measured it and probed it.
He said to man,
"See! Fear of the Lord is wisdom;
To shun evil is understanding."
(28:23–28)

Wisdom, then, means fearing (and obeying) God. Only foolish people try to get through life on their own because human wisdom is partial and flawed. This is also the message of Proverbs, but the structure of statement and counterstatement is much more sophisticated than anything in the Proverbs. It surpasses nearly every other short poem in the Bible in the complexity of both its structure and its argument. It is, in other words, a very good poem.

But what is it doing in Job? It seems to come from nowhere. In one chapter, Job is insulting his friends and shaking his fist at God, and in the next chapter he (or somebody) recites a complex lyrical ode that has nothing to do with anything that has come before it. This is not the most perplexing textual problem in the Book of Job, but it ranks pretty high on the list. Clearly, somebody, at some point in the editing process, thought that this poem belonged in Job. And I think they were absolutely right.

The Hymn to Wisdom does not fit very well into the Job story. Nobody we meet in the previous chapters (3–27) could possibly speak these words, which contradict the arguments of both Job and his Comforters. But this is precisely what makes chapter 28 valuable: it shows us the common flaw in everybody else's reasoning. Job's Comforters believe that they understand why God has made Job suffer. Job does not understand why he suffers, but he thinks he should be able to find out. He honestly believes that God owes him an explanation. Underneath the assertions of Job, Eliphaz, Bildad, and Zophar lurks the unquestioned assumption that humans should be able to understand the ways of God.

The main point of the Hymn to Wisdom, on the other hand, is that God understands some things (collectively called "Wisdom") that human beings can never understand. God has a perspective that we lack. He "sees to the ends of the earth [and] observes all that is beneath the heavens." When Job and his friends try to understand God's reasoning, they must always fail because they do not have access to the divine perspective. Unlike God, they have never "fixed the weight of the winds," "set the measure of the waters," or "made a rule for the rain." As the creator of the world and everything in it, God has an understanding that His creations simply can't ever share. It is no accident that this is also the core assertion of the Elihu chapters or that, when God finally does deign to speak to Job, He will communicate many of the same things.

Job's Final Speech

When the Hymn to Wisdom ends, the text reverts briefly to prose, just a single line, that says, "Job again took up his theme and said" (29:1). This brief line of introduction signals a return to the main story arc of the poem. Unlike the Hymn to Wisdom, which precedes it, or the speeches of Elihu, which follow it, Job's final speech in chapters 29 through 31 was almost certainly part of the original poem. It functions as the rhetorical bridge that takes us from the Wisdom dialogue to God's final answer. At least one modern poetic translation of Job, Stephen Mitchell's 1979 stand-alone *The Book of Job*, restores this order of the text by omitting the Wisdom hymn and the Elihu chapters. The result is an elegant, extremely coherent literary text that presents the Book of Job as it may well have appeared to its original readers.

Like the Hymn to Wisdom, Job's final speech includes three chapter-length segments that are organized very loosely on the same three-part structure of the hymn. In the first (chapter 29), Job recalls the good life he had before his misfortunes began. In the second (chapter 30), he surveys the miseries and indignities of his current situation. And in the third (chapter 31), he gives a final accounting of his life and declares himself innocent of any sin that could have occasioned God's displeasure.

In the first part of his speech, Job longs to be "as in months gone by, / In the days when God watched over me, / When His lamp shone over my head, / When I walked in the dark by its light" (29:2–3). This portion of the speech brims with Job's nostalgia for his life of ease and prosperity—a time when "my feet were bathed in cream / And rocks poured out streams of oil for me" (29:6). But Job does not spend the bulk of the chapter pining for his great wealth, or even for his children or his own health. The thing he misses most, judging from his own report, is the respect he enjoyed in his community:

> When I passed through the city gates
> To take my seat in the square,
> Young men saw me and hid,
> Elders rose and stood;

Nobles held back their words;
They clapped their hands to their mouths.
The voices of princes were hushed;
Their tongues stuck to their palates.

. . .

Men would listen to me expectantly,
And wait for my counsel.
After I spoke they had nothing to say;
My words were as drops [of dew] upon them.
They waited for me as for rain,
For the late rain, their mouths open wide.
(29:7–10; 21–23)

Job does not say so directly, but he provides enough information for us to understand that this great respect flowed from his great wealth. His wealth, in turn, flowed from God's favor—which, he insists in this final speech, he deserved because of his righteous life. "I clothed myself in righteousness and it robed me" (29:14), he recalls, "I was eyes to the blind / And feet to the lame; / I was a father to the needy, / And I looked into the case of the stranger" (29:15–16). Given God's own words in the frame, we can have no doubt that Job is correct. He was a superlatively good man, and he was a superlatively wealthy man—and he clearly saw the former as the cause of the latter. Quite logically, he muses, "I thought, I would end my days with my family, and be as long-lived as the phoenix" (29:18).

With one very important exception, the second part of Job's final speech reverses everything in the first part. Whereas he once commanded the respect of everyone he met, "now those younger than I deride me." Of the men who once feared him, he says, "they abhor me; they keep their distance from me; / They do not withhold spittle from my face" (30:1, 10). His once towering figure has been reduced to abject misery, and God, who once lifted Job up above all other men, now "has regarded me as clay / [and] I have become like dust and ashes" (30:19).

From his perspective, Job has gone from blessed, wealthy, and respected to cursed, impoverished, and reviled. But the one thing has not changed is his belief in his own righteousness. And this is what torments him the most. According to everything he has always believed, "blessed, wealthy, and respected" are the natural consequences of righteousness, while "cursed, impoverished, and reviled" are the direct result of sin. "Did I not weep for the unfortunate?" he asks, "Did I not grieve for the needy? I looked forward to good fortune, but evil came; / I hoped for light, but darkness came" (30:25–26).

The contrast between what Job has experienced and what he feels he has the right to expect sets up the third and final segment of his speech, in which he declares himself innocent of any sin that could possibly have caused his suffering. This declaration has much in common with the Egyptian "negative confession" text found in the Papyrus of Ani and other funerary scrolls.[3] But it is also consistent with Jewish law, which allowed a defendant to take a solemn oath of innocence, after which his accuser had to produce proof or drop the charges (see Exodus 22:11; 1 Kings 8:31–32). This provision of the Law almost certainly motivates Job's solemn oath of innocence, which reads, in part:

> I never saw an unclad wretch,
> A needy man without clothing,
> Whose loins did not bless me
> As he warmed himself with the shearings of my sheep.
> If I raised my hand against the fatherless,
> Looking to my supporters in the gate,
> May my arm drop off my shoulder;
> My forearm break off at the elbow.
> For I am in dread of God-sent calamity;
> I cannot bear His threat.
> (31:19–23)

Theologically, this list looks more like the Sermon on the Mount than anything else in the Old Testament. It says nothing about performing sacrifices or engaging in any other ritual, nor does it even mention staying away from idols or refusing to worship graven images. Rather, it focuses on the kind of other-directed ethical code that we now associate with New Testament Christianity: caring for the poor, comforting the afflicted, and protecting the most vulnerable members of society. Both what Job includes in his declaration, and what he excludes in it, tell us much about the ethical principles that the Job poet considered important—and they

---

3. In his *Anchor Bible* commentary, Marvin Pope writes that "Job's repudiation of evil here has been compared to the negative confession in the Egyptian Book of the Dead in which the deceased facing the final judgment before Osiris enumerates the long list of sins he has not committed. . . . The similarities are striking, but not sufficient to indicate direct interdependence. Both catalogues of sin reflect high ideals of social ethics. The Egyptian list is a mixture of ethical and ritual concerns, while Job's, with one exception [31:26–28] is entirely ethical" (227).

are very different than the things that the Priestly and Deuteronomistic writers in the same historical moment chose to focus upon.[4]

Ultimately, however, the character Job has still not reached the ethical understanding of the poet telling the story. For all the other-directed focus of his ethical framework, he acknowledges that he did all of these good things because "I am in dread of God-sent calamity." The fear of punishment that Job credits for his ethical behavior here is simply the flipside of the expectation of reward that he acknowledges in the previous two chapters. In his own closing speech, then, Job characterizes his fabled righteousness as a form of enlightened self-interest—an attempt to curry favor with God in order to procure rewards and avoid punishments. Let us not forget that this is exactly what Satan said about Job in the prologue.

Along Comes Elihu

Scholars have long considered Elihu to be the sore thumb of the Book of Job—not least because he interrupts the flow of the narrative right when it is getting good. Everything in the Job poem—its language, its structure, and its rhetoric—builds to the fantastic crescendo when Yahweh himself appears on the scene to answer Job's charges. And just at the moment that the revelation becomes inevitable, Elihu appears on the scene and spends six chapters (32–37) unilaterally refuting Job's arguments in the Wisdom dialogue. For thousands of years, readers and commentators have viewed Elihu's speech the way we might view a thirty-minute infomercial before the climax of a suspenseful movie.

Almost everything in the Elihu chapters sticks out from the rest of the story. When he interrupts the narrative, he seems to appear from nowhere, claiming that he had heard the entire dialogue (somehow managing to remain hidden from all four participants while doing so) and feels compelled to respond. When he does, he gives a six-chapter monologue instead of the dialogue we have become accustomed to. Neither Job nor his friends respond to anything that Elihu says, nor does any character do or say anything at any time to acknowledge Elihu's presence in the text.

Scholars of the Old Testament almost unanimously consider Elihu a later addition to the Job manuscript. Too much about this section goes against the grain of the original narrative, and too much of what he says assumes a knowledge of God's final speech. This does not mean, however,

---

4. David Bokovoy, *Authoring the Old Testament: Genesis–Deuteronomy*, 42–51, 62–70.

that critics unanimously dismiss what Elihu has to say. Quite the reverse: as Carol Newsom argues in *The Book of Job: A Contest of Moral Imaginations* (2003), reading Elihu's speeches as secondary texts has the advantage of "opening up the text to interpretive issues much richer and more nuanced than those available on the assumption that the Elihu speeches are part of the original design."[5] Elihu may not tell us anything about what the original poet intended, but he can tell us a lot about how ancient Jews read the Book of Job, which is equally important to our understanding of the text.

And there can be no doubt that Elihu's commentary comes from a Jewish perspective, as his name (Hebrew for "My God is Yahweh") is the only recognizably Jewish proper noun in the entire Book of Job. The author of the original Job poem takes great pains to present Job and his Comforters as universal Everyman characters whose experiences include, but transcend the Jewish experience. Unlike the other names in Job, which do not occur anywhere else in the Hebrew canon, "Elihu" appears four other places in the Old Testament (1 Samuel 1:1; 1 Chronicles 12:20, 26:7, 27:18). This gives us some important clues about how Elihu's speeches ended up in the Book of Job, as it suggests the possibility that the original readers wanted it to be more recognizably Jewish.

We can best read the Elihu monologue, I believe, as a series of annotations in the margin—notes from an ancient reader scribbled in the corners of the Job manuscript, reframing and strengthening the Comforters' arguments and responding directly to things that Job says. Every sincere reader of Job should have such notes—for as Newsom points out, Elihu comes to the text of Job the way that we all do. "The reader," she argues, "always comes to a conversation that has begun without him and yet at which he finds himself present, a conversation that engages him and yet has no place for him." We too must try to engage Job and his Comforters in some kind of dialogue, even though the communication will always be one way.[6]

In the first chapter of his speech (chapter 32), Elihu does not even address Job. Rather, he criticizes the Comforters for not defending their positions well enough and for allowing Job to besmirch God's good name. He held back out of respect for their age, but after hearing how incompetently they refuted Job's arguments, he feels compelled to speak. "I saw that none of you could argue with Job," he says to nobody in particular. "I too would like to hold forth, / For I am full of words" (32:12, 17–18). And hold forth he does. By the time that Elihu finishes his speech at

5. Carol Newsom, *The Book of Job: A Contest of Moral Imaginations*, 201.
6. Ibid., 202.

the end of chapter 37, we can be reasonably certain that every argument against Job's position has been made clearly, directly, and systematically by someone who does not know Job and has no interest in preserving a relationship with him. Unlike the Comforters, whose arguments arose organically through the give and take of a dialogue, Elihu simply delivers a rebuttal to a static body of assertions. As he announces up front, his only purpose in doing so is to defend the honor of God. And he begins with the Comforter's argument that Job cannot be guiltless because God would not allow an innocent person to suffer:

> Therefore, men of understanding, listen to me;
> Wickedness be far from God,
> Wrongdoing, from Shaddai!
> For He pays a man according to his actions,
> And provides for him according to his conduct;
> For God surely does not act wickedly;
> Shaddai does not pervert justice.
> (34:10–12)

Like the Comforters, Elihu simply refuses to believe that "one who hates justice" governs the universe (34:17). The consequence of a God who does not follow understandable ethical rules is too terrible for him to contemplate.

In a sense, however, he does contemplate it—or at least he contemplates a defense of God that does not rule out actions that humans consider unjust. Throughout his monologue, Elihu develops a line of argument that the Comforters only hint at (see 15:7–8): God cannot be judged by human standards of right and wrong because He operates from a perspective that we do not have access to:

> Indeed, you have stated in my hearing,
> I heard the words spoken,
> "I am guiltless, free from transgression;
> I am innocent, without iniquity.
> But He finds reasons to oppose me,
> Considers me His enemy.
> He puts my feet in stocks,
> Watches all my ways."
> In this you are not right;
> I will answer you: God is greater than any man.
> Why do you complain against Him
> That He does not reply to any of man's charges?
> (33:8–13)

This is an extremely effective answer to Job, as it allows for the possibility that Job may be as innocent as he says he is and yet may still be suffering for reasons that (not being God) he cannot understand. Elihu does here what the most effective debaters always do: he goes beneath the actual argument, finds the underlying assumption, and attacks it instead. Under the terms of this argument, Job's innocence need not cast doubt on God's justice because God himself is beyond human understanding:

> See, God is beyond reach in His power;
> Who governs like Him?
> Who ever reproached Him for His conduct?
> Who ever said, "You have done wrong"?
> Remember, then, to magnify His work,
> Of which men have sung,
> Which all men have beheld,
> Men have seen, from a distance.
> See, God is greater than we can know;
> The number of His years cannot be counted.
> (36:22–26)

This line of reasoning foreshadows the argument that God himself will implicitly make through questions that he asks Job in His own speech. As Elihu continues, his arguments sound more and more like God's—perhaps suggesting that the redactor who added the speech felt some responsibility to provide a transition back into the poem that he interrupted. In fact, in the final chapter of his speech, Elihu uses many of the same rhetorical devices that God uses immediately thereafter. He points to the awesome majesty of the natural world, explains God's role in that majesty, and then asks Job, in effect, if he can play in the same league as God:

> Causing each of them to happen to His land,
> Whether as a scourge or as a blessing.
> Give ear to this, Job;
> Stop to consider the marvels of God.
> Do you know what charge God lays upon them
> When His lightning-clouds shine?
> Do you know the marvels worked upon the expanse of clouds
> By Him whose understanding is perfect,
> Why your clothes become hot
> When the land is becalmed by the south wind?
> Can you help him stretch out the heavens,
> Firm as a mirror of cast metal?
> (37:13–18)

Though nearly all scholars believe that the Elihu chapters were added to the Job manuscript after its original author or authors completed their work, there is no general agreement about why. Some have argued that the insertion was made by a pious Jew who wanted to blunt the potential for blasphemy in some of Job's speeches. Others suggest that it was inserted by a member of the Joban school who wanted to make sure that the poem accounted for every possible argument against Job's position. And at least one well-known biblical scholar argues that the original Job poet added the Elihu speeches some time after completing the original manuscript to clarify and perhaps correct his original intentions.[7]

Many scholars believe that Elihu's speeches, while secondary, create a valuable transition between the Wisdom dialogue and God's response. Brevard Childs frames this transition theologically, arguing that "Elihu uses the theme of divine discipline in an attempt to force Job out of the theological dilemma of assuming that, if God does not recognize his innocence, God is either lacking in justice or power." This, in turn, provides "the climactic hermeneutical link between the speeches and the divine response." Samuel Terrien frames it much more poetically. Elihu's monologue "prepares the hero—and the reader—for hearing the Voice from the Whirlwind. . . . It constitutes a threshold—however imperfect—to the Holy of Holies."[8]

Read together with the Hymn to Wisdom, the speeches of Elihu suggest that the earliest readers of Job—perhaps after a fair amount of debate with each other—coalesced around an interpretation of the text that required them to condemn neither Job (which would have been difficult to reconcile with the poet's intentions) or God (which would have been theologically unthinkable). The easiest way out of this dilemma, which is fully consistent with the Hebrew understanding of God, declares Yahweh beyond human understanding and, therefore, human definitions of good and evil. This is actually a very plausible interpretation of the questions that God asks in his final speech, and it remains one of the most common ways to interpret the final section of Job. It is not, however, the only way to interpret God's answer. As we will see in the next chapter, the history of the final scene's reception includes interpretations much less complimentary to both Job and God.

I think it likely—though I certainly can't prove it—that the earliest Jewish readers of Job admired the poem and approved of its message but

---

7. Robert Gordis, "Elihu the Intruder," 69–71.

8. Brevard S. Childs, *Introduction to the Old Testament as Scripture*, 541; Samuel Terrien, *Job: The Poet of Existence*, 190.

feared that others might side too much with Job and be tempted to see his suffering as a criticism of God. When God answers Job, he does so with questions; he never makes a declarative statement like, "I am beyond your comprehension, so stop trying to fit me into your puny human categories of good and evil." Without such a statement, we have the latitude to impute a whole range of possible meanings to God's final answer. But we find exactly these kinds of declarative statements in both the Hymn to Wisdom and in the speeches of Elihu. By placing these two texts on either side of Job's final declaration, and before the appearance of Yahweh, the unknown editor ingeniously constrains our interpretation of both sets of speeches.

Chapter Six

God (Sort of) Answers Job
(38–42:6)

*There can be no doubt that behind all the actions of this court of jus-
tice, that is to say in my case, behind my arrest and today's interroga-
tion, there is a great organization at work. An organization which
not only employs corrupt warders, oafish Inspectors, and Examining
Magistrates . . . . And the significance of this great organization,
gentlemen? It consists in this, that innocent persons are accused of
guilt, and senseless proceedings are put in motion against them.*
                                        —Franz Kafka, *The Trial*

You Call This an Answer?

No writer has ever tried harder to understand Job than Franz Kafka.
In one way or another, all of Kafka's major works attempt to inhabit the
world from the Job's-eye view of a man struggling in vain with powerful
forces that he can neither predict nor control. And nothing in Kafka's
collected work brings us closer to our story than *The Trial*, which, as
Northrup Frye writes, "reads like a kind of 'midrash' on the Book of Job."[1]
The anti-hero of *The Trial*, Joseph K., is arrested one morning for an un-
disclosed crime and told that he must prepare a defense. Throughout the
novel, he tries in vain to discover what he stands accused of so he can
defend himself, but he never learns. The judicial proceedings have nothing
to do with justice, only with power, and at the end of the novel he is taken
out and executed "like a dog."[2]
Once we factor out 2,500 years of history and a fair amount of
Modernist angst, Job's story is essentially the same. Job loses — in rapid
succession — his family, his property, and his health in ways that both he

---

1. Northrup Frye, *The Great Code*, 195.
2. Franz Kafka, *The Trial*, 229.

and his friends believe to be a sign of God's disfavor. His friends urge him to repent, but Job has no idea what he should repent of. Over and over again, he asks God to tell him what he has done wrong so he can defend himself, but God does not answer. Readers of the frame understand God's bet with Satan, and astute readers of the poem know that the poet wants us to question the entire theological apparatus of rewards and punishments. But all Job knows is that the most powerful entity in the universe wants to squish him like a bug.

Unlike Joseph K., however, Job does get an answer from God. Sort of. At least God addresses Job at the end of the poem. And, as Robert Alter reports, He does so in some of the most beautiful and powerful constructions ever created in the Hebrew language:

> If the poetry of Job . . . looms above all other biblical poetry in virtuosity and sheer expressive power, the culminating poem that God speaks out of the storm soars beyond everything that has preceded it in the book, the poet having wrought a poetic idiom even richer and more awesome than the one he gave Job. Through this pushing of poetic expression towards its own upper limits, the concluding speech helps us see the panorama of creation, as perhaps we could do only through poetry, with the eyes of God.[3]

While scholars have long marveled at the power of God's poetry, they have been less than impressed with the helpfulness of His answers. Rather than allowing Job to question Him, God demands the opportunity to question Job. God thunders from the storm that signifies His presence, "Who is this who darkens counsel / speaking without knowledge? / Gird your loins like a man; / I will ask and you will inform Me" (38:2–3). And the questions that God puts to Job are all some variation of either "Do you know what I know?" or "Can you do what I can do?"

> Where were you when I laid the earth's foundations?
> Speak if you have understanding.
> Do you know who fixed its dimensions
> Or who measured it with a line?
> Onto what were its bases sunk?
> Who set its cornerstone
> When the morning stars sang together
> And all the divine beings shouted for joy?
> Who closed the sea behind doors
> When it gushed forth out of the womb,
> When I clothed it in clouds,

---

3. Robert Alter, *The Art of Biblical Poetry*, 87.

Swaddled it in dense clouds,
When I made breakers My limit for it,
And set up its bar and doors,
And said, "You may come so far and no farther;
Here your surging waves will stop"?
Have you ever commanded the day to break,
Assigned the dawn its place,
So that it seizes the corners of the earth
And shakes the wicked out of it?
It changes like clay under the seal
Till [its hues] are fixed like those of a garment.
Their light is withheld from the wicked,
And the upraised arm is broken.
(38:4–15)

And so on. In question after question, God forces Job to confront the sheer awesomeness of His power. God knows when the mountain goats give birth (39:1), He tells the eagle when to soar (39:27), and He can make the horse quiver like locusts (39:20). God has immense and marvelous power, but Job has known this all along. He said right at the start that he could never win an argument with one "who performs great deeds which cannot be fathomed" (9:10). Job has always acknowledged God's awesome power; what he wanted was some awesome justice—which, it turns out, has nothing to do with making horses quiver.

Many readers of Job have found it difficult to defend God's responses because they do nothing to answer Job's questions. "Few speeches in all of literature can more properly be called overpowering than the Lord's speeches to Job from the whirlwind," writes Jack Miles. "But therein lies all their difficulty. The Lord refers to absolutely nothing about himself except his power."[4] Robert Alter paraphrases God's answer as, "If you can't begin to play in My league, you should not have the nerve to ask questions about the rules of the game."[5]

Nobody has ever been harder on Job's God than the great psychologist Carl Jung, who wrote an entire book on the last four chapters of Job and concluded that Yahweh has serious psychological issues:

For seventy-one verses he proclaims his world creating power to his miserable victim, who sits in ashes and scratches his sores with potsherds, and who by now has had more than enough of superhuman violence. Job has absolutely

---

4. Jack Miles, *God: A Biography*, 314.
5. Alter, *The Art of Biblical Poetry*, 86.

no need of being impressed by further exhibitions of this power. . . . His thunderings at Job so completely miss the point that one cannot help but see how much he is occupied with himself.[6]

In Jung's analysis, God's failure to respond appropriately to Job becomes the central event of the Christian Bible, for it forces Yahweh to acknowledge the moral superiority of one of His own creations and, in response, to take on human form in the person of Jesus Christ. "Job stands morally higher than Yahweh. In this respect the creature has surpassed the creator," Jung writes. "Yahweh must become man precisely because he has done man a wrong. He, the guardian of justice, knows that every wrong must be expiated. . . . Because his creature has surpassed him he must regenerate himself." He must take, not only the form of a human, but also the form of a suffering human so that, through his own suffering, he can atone for the suffering that he caused another.[7]

Jung reinterprets Job as a counterpoint to the story of the Fall of Adam—but with a twist. In Job, God is the one who falls. Yahweh, not Adam, commits the original sin and creates the need for reconciliation. God creates the gap between Himself and humanity that the Atonement must bridge. And His sin has nothing to do with disobedience, or forbidden fruit, or even sex. God falls from His own grace when He causes an innocent person to suffer in order to accomplish a selfish goal. He treats Job as an instrument of his own pleasure and not as a morally significant being worthy of respect. As in Job God died, so also in Christ will God be made alive.

The connections that Jung forges between Job and Jesus Christ only make sense if we accept the whole Jungian model of the "collective unconscious"—a great storehouse of primal archetypes that we all draw upon to create myths and legends. In such a model, "God" and "Job" are local manifestations of deeper, more fundamental archetypes whose essential characteristics are hardwired into the human mind. One such archetype, according to Jung, is the story of a morally evolving god who voluntarily submits to mortality in order to reconcile Himself to his creations.

The Role of Revelation

God's arguments in this final scene are notoriously hard to pin down because they consist almost entirely of questions, which can only be turned

---

6. C. G. Jung, *God's Answer to Job*, 16.
7. Ibid., 43.

into answers with the application of a fair bit of interpretive spin. Jung's interpretation assumes that we should spin God's rhetorical questions as statements that read something like, "How dare you ask me why you are suffering when you are an inferior little vermin who isn't even worth the time it would take to kill you quickly?" But God never actually says this, or anything remotely like this, and the text itself will support much less antagonistic interpretations of the final scene.

For example, we can spin God's speech positively by simply pointing out that, for all of His divine grumbling, God actually does talk to Job—and at some length too. In a sense, His actions refute His arguments. If He had really been too busy lassoing whales and moving mountains to listen to one man's problems, then He would never have bothered to show up at all. Robert Alter takes this view when he writes, "The moment the Voice begins to address Job out of the storm, Job already has his answer: that, despite appearances to the contrary, God cares enough about man to reveal Himself to humankind."[8]

This line of interpretation has special resonance for Latter-day Saints, as it underscores both the need for, and the availability of, continuing divine revelation. John Tanner makes this point in his 1990 article, "Why Latter-day Saints Should Read Job." The Book of Job, he argues, "is at bottom about the need for revelation. Revelation is the key to human crises of faith brought on by suffering. This interpretation . . . fits our theology which stresses the need for both general and personal revelation." "That the Lord responds at all," Tanner concludes, "assures us that he is not a *deus absconditus*, as Job fears . . . but a God who condescends to reveal himself to us in our darkest hours of need."[9]

But just what does God tell Job? The mere presence of a divine being does not constitute revelation. Something also has to be revealed, some truth articulated, or some new knowledge created—otherwise it's just a visit. But clearly God wants to communicate something to Job, and by the end of the poem Job seems to feel that his questions have been answered. If we assume that God does more in this final scene than just browbeat Job into submitting to His superior power (which would be pointless, since Job submits to God's superior power long before the scene begins), then we need to look around for possible revelatory messages in God's questions.

---

8. Alter, *The Art of Biblical Poetry*, 87.
9. John S. Tanner, "Why Latter-Day Saints Should Read Job," 45–46.

One common modern interpretation of God's answer is related by Harvard President James B. Conant in his 1952 book, *Modern Science and Modern Man*. "If I read the book of Job correctly," he explains, "its lesson is a denial of the assumption that the universe is explicable in human terms; it is a corrective to the presumption of human beings in applying their standards of value to the cosmos."[10] Since at least the eighteenth century, this reading of Job has provided a counterweight to the Enlightenment narrative of science as a force that can, and eventually will, unravel all of the universe's mysteries.

But no such narrative existed when our poet first wrote Job. Nobody in the ancient world thought that they could understand the universe through a process of observation and hypothesis testing. But they did think that they could understand it through inductive reasoning and magic. They believed—as humans have always believed—that they could generalize from their own experiences to create universal principles that allowed them to control their environment. The law of retribution is one such principle. The law of gravity is another. And behind both of these laws lurks a human nature supremely uncomfortable with randomness.

God's answer to Job tells us that we had better learn how to be comfortable with a random universe, or at least with a universe that we perceive as random, because we will never have anything else. God's questions force Job to confront the immensity of a universe in which he, Job, is only an infinitesimally small part. Minimally, God's answer supports a stoic recognition that since we will never understand why things happen, we might as well stop making ourselves miserable and do the best that we can with the resources we have. Such a recognition would not be without its comforts to those who suffer from anxiety thinking that they can predict or control the universe.

The world that God shows Job is random to Job, but it is not random to God. Job's God is not a *deus abscondus*, or even a Clockmaker God who lets the world run according to the rules He created. He is an obsessive micromanager who supervises every part of His creation at an excruciating level of detail. Job, and all sufferers, can take comfort in the idea that God understands how our stories fit into the much grander narratives of infinity and eternity—even if we do not. Theologian and scholar Emil Kraeling applies this argument to Job in his major work, *The Book of the Ways of God*:

> God, so the poet would have us realize, has infinite power, but He also has a purpose, which His power serves. The existence of such a purpose must

---

10. Nahum N. Glatzer, *The Dimensions of Job*, 247.

not be questioned, because we cannot discern it at every point. We see so much of it in the great arrangements of the world that we must believe in its existence where our understanding fails us.[11]

This interpretation aligns the ending of the poem with the ending of the frame. If the ultimate message of the poem is "God will work everything out in His own time," then Job's great rewards in the end make sense. In fact, if we accept the frame tale's epilogue as the poet's preferred ending for Job, then such a reading becomes inevitable. But even if we read the epilogue ironically (as I believe we should), we can still discern in God's final speech the argument that humans can never understand divine justice because humanness cannot transcend the profound bias it experiences toward its own point of view.

This interpretation leads to an understanding of Job as a poem about having faith in God—not because God rewards the faithful with great gifts, but because He is a God worth having faith in. When we interpret them charitably, God's questions seem designed to convince Job that He, God, sees connection and purpose where Job sees only randomness and disorder. Job has drawn conclusions about God's justice on the basis of the very limited example of his own suffering. Perhaps the most important thing that God has to do in his speech is convince Job that his sample size is too small by an order of infinity.

Behemoth and Leviathan

Strictly speaking, God gives two speeches to Job in the finale. The first speech in chapters 38 and 39 consists of the series of questions we have been discussing so far. At the end of these questions, Job acquiesces to the force of God's power, if not the strength of His argument:

> See, I am of small worth; what can I answer You?
> I clap my hand to my mouth.
> I have spoken once, and will not reply;
> Twice, and will do so no more.
> (40:4–5)

From this point on, Yahweh radically shifts rhetorical strategies. Instead of firing off questions about seemingly random parts of the universe that Job knows nothing about, He focuses on two mythical beasts that Job's readers had probably heard of but had almost certainly never seen: Behemoth and

---

11. Emil G. Kraeling, "A Theodicy—and More," 211.

Leviathan. Textual critics have suggested that the former is based loosely on the hippopotamus, while the latter comes from common descriptions of the crocodile—both animals that had been captured and displayed in Egypt and spoken of in hushed tones throughout the ancient Near East. God describes the first of these beasts, Behemoth, in such frankly sexual terms that translators have hidden behind euphemism for thousands of years:

> Take now behemoth, whom I made as I did you;
> He eats grass, like the cattle.
> His strength is in his loins,
> His might in the muscles of his belly.
> He makes his tail stand up like a cedar;
> The sinews of his thighs are knit together.
> His bones are like tubes of bronze,
> His limbs like iron rods.
> (40:15–18)

Behemoth's primary attribute is his frank sexual power: the "virile strength" in his belly, the "sinews of his thighs" (i.e., his testicles), and his "tail" (almost certainly a phallic euphemism) standing like a cedar. This description earns every word of the Freudian interpretations often given him by commentators such as Rabbi Kushner, who remarks:

> Behemoth is the Primal Life force that gives people the energy to do things and to have an impact on the lives of other people for good or ill. Thousands of years from now, a man named Sigmund Freud will call it Id and Eros. Part of it is sexual. That is the significance of the priapic male organ referred to in 40:16. That part of it is probably responsible for more happiness and more pain, more joy and more anguish, than anything else in [the] universe.[12]

We do not have to accept too much of the Freudian paradigm to agree with Kushner that 1) God describes Behemoth in extremely sexual terms; and 2) the text presents that sexuality as something both magnificent and potentially destructive. Indeed, for a description of the entire Hebrew Bible's attitude toward sexuality, one could do much worse than to describe it, as the Job poet describes Behemoth: a magnificent and powerful thing that must be carefully controlled to prevent it from becoming destructive.

Significantly, when discussing Behemoth, God turns away from his rhetorical strategy of asking Job questions that he cannot answer. Instead, He merely describes the creature and explains how He has contained its potentially disruptive sexuality: "He lies down beneath the lotuses, / In the cover

---

12. Harold Kushner, *When Bad Things Happen to Good People*, 149–50.

of the swamp reeds. / The lotuses embower him with shade, / The willows of the brook surround him" (40:21–22). By "embowering" Behemoth, the poet symbolically contains Behemoth's sexual power the way that it should be contained: in a traditional symbol of marriage (the bridal bower). Robert Alter translates the first part of verse 22 even more intriguingly as "the lotus hedges him"—which immediately connects Behemoth to Job—the other character in the poem who has been "hedged in" by God.[13]

God, then, has contained Behemoth as He has contained Job. This gives Job yet another example of how hard God works to keep everything running, but it also establishes Behemoth as a kind of analogy to Job—a creature kept at bay for reasons that God understands clearly but the creature understands not at all. We need not press this analogy too far. Job is not exactly an embodiment of smoldering sexuality. But, like Behemoth, Job is a creature who must be made to acknowledge the superiority of the Creator's perspective.

The second creature that God refers to builds on the idea of a dangerous beast that must be controlled. But the power of Leviathan is much more destructive than creative. Leviathan—based loosely on a crocodile but really more like a sea monster or a dragon—is one of the scariest mythical beasts that a poet could have introduced into an ancient poem. The poet devotes the whole of chapter 41 to describing the terrors of the mighty Leviathan—terrors that far exceed those of any normal crocodile.

We learn, for example, that he is a fire-breather: "His sneezings flash lightning," "firebrands stream from his mouth" and "out of his nostrils comes smoke / As from a steaming, boiling cauldron" (41:10–12). And we learn that his power exceeds that of all other creatures: "Strength resides in his neck; / Power leaps before him" (41:14), "his heart is cast hard as a stone" (41:16). But most importantly, we learn that nobody can tame this fearsome beast. "Divine beings are in dread as he rears up," the poet stresses. "No sword that overtakes him can prevail, / nor spear, nor missile, nor lance. / He regards iron as straw, / Bronze as rotted wood. / No arrow can put him to flight; / Slingstones turn into stubble for him" (41:17–20).

In much the same way that Behemoth embodies sexuality, Leviathan embodies violence—and, in particular, the impunity that comes with being able to inflict violence without fear of consequence, since no force on earth can contain Leviathan's power. But God can contain it, and at the

---

13. Robert Alter, *The Wisdom Books: Job, Proverbs, and Ecclesiastes: A Translation with Commentary*, 170. See also Alter's translation of Job 3:23 on page 21.

end of chapter 40, before going on to describe Leviathan, God reverts briefly to the strategy of asking Job questions designed to showcase His ability (and Job's inability) to deal with Leviathan's threat:

> Can you draw out Leviathan by a fishhook?
> Can you press down his tongue by a rope?
> Can you put a ring through his nose,
> Or pierce his jaw with a barb?
> Will he plead with you at length?
> Will he speak soft words to you?
> Will he make an agreement with you
> To be taken as your lifelong slave?
> Will you play with him like a bird,
> And tie him down for your girls?
> (40:25–29)

Here, in just a few verses, the fiercest monster imaginable becomes a child's plaything. Leviathan is more inherently threatening than Behemoth, but his power is contained more completely. Thus, when God goes on to describe the terrors of the monster, Job (like the reader) already understands that those terrors have been completely domesticated in a way that God understands and Job cannot fathom.

God presents both the fearsome sexuality of Behemoth and the raw violent power of Leviathan as dangerous, potentially destabilizing, and difficult to control. He does not, however, use any kind of moral vocabulary to describe them. They are not "evil" or "wicked." They do not disobey God or reject his dominion. They are, rather, forces of nature that God created because he wanted them in His world. Though they can both inflict tremendous damage to other parts of God's creation (particularly human beings), such damage does not have a moral dimension. It is simply a consequence of the way that God created the world.

This contrasts markedly from the world that Job imagines when he petitions God for an audience. In Job's world, the only standard for moral judgment is the effect that something has on human beings—and particularly on Job. Something is "good" if it makes Job happy and "bad" if it makes him sad. If something bad has happened to Job, then, he and all of his friends must try to figure out what bad thing he did to deserve it. He must have done something; otherwise, God would not be just. Such neat and simplistic philosophies cannot exist side by side with the awesome, but completely amoral power of Behemoth and Leviathan.

Getting the Question Right

Whether we read the end of the Job poem positively (as God reassuring Job that He's got everything covered) or negatively (as God browbeating Job into submission with a crass demonstration of His power), we need to be sure that we read it as a poem and not as an actual historical dialogue. When we understand Job's God as a literary character—one designed to fulfill a narrative function rather than create a theologically defensible image of divine power—then we can start asking the kinds of questions likely to lead, if not to secure knowledge, then at least to actual wisdom.

The most important of these questions is "Why does God talk to Job in the first place?" By this, I do not mean the theological question, "Why would God appear to somebody like Job?" This question assumes a historical, rather than a literary text. I also do not mean the artistic question, "Why would the poet want to end the Job poem with the words of God?" The entire poem builds up to the final moment of revelation, so it would make no sense for it to end any other way than it does. But God still needs a motive, which is to say that the poet has to create a reason for God to take the unusual step of coming down to earth in the form of a storm and asking a lot of rhetorical questions to a suffering mortal.

Most of the commentary I have quoted here suggest that God's purpose is to answer Job's questions. Those who fault God for not giving Job a good answer assume that Job has asked God a good question—something like, "Why do I have to suffer?" But the question Job actually asks is, "What did I do to cause you to make me suffer?" This is a very different question because it builds in assumptions about God's motives and about the way the universe works. Any answer that God gives Job would confirm these underlying assumptions, so God does not try to answer at all. It is simply the Ancient Hebrew version of "Have you stopped beating your wife yet?"

Job's entire claim to God's attention rests on this incorrect assumption. In the last words of his final speech, he directly invokes his legal rights as an accused person to confront his accuser:

> O that I had someone to give me a hearing;
> O that Shaddai would reply to my writ,
> Or my accuser draw up a true bill!
> I would carry it on my shoulder;
> Tie it around me for a wreath.
> I would give him an account of my steps,
> Offer it as to a commander.
> (31:35–37)

When Yahweh appears in the storm, however, he rejects Job's right to question him and demands that Job submit to His questions. We might possibly read this as an example of God bullying Job, or as a claim of immunity from questioning based on His being the creator of the universe. But when God begins his second round of questions, He makes it clear that He is asking the questions because *He* is the one accused of wrongdoing:

> Gird your loins like a man;
> I will ask, and you will inform Me.
> Would you impugn My justice?
> Would you condemn Me that you may be right?
> (40:7–8)

God does not intend to answer Job's questions. Rather, he will answer Job's accusations. God appears in order to acquit Himself of the charge that He acted unjustly—not to give Job a lecture on the metaphysics of suffering.

By switching the roles of accuser and accused, the poet forces us to reconsider all of the assumptions that have governed the poem up to this point. Most of the speeches in Job reflect one of two seemingly contradictory positions: 1) Job's argument that he has done nothing to deserve his suffering and that God is therefore unjust; or 2) the Comforters' argument that God is inherently just and that Job must therefore have done something to deserve his suffering. In the final scene, however, it becomes clear that both arguments are essentially the same: they both assume that God's justice has something to do with Job's happiness. When He finally appears to speak for Himself, God acts as though He has never even considered such a thing.

Job's speeches do not just accuse God of injustice, however. They also accuse Him of incompetence—of making a mistake in punishing the obviously innocent Job. In the Wisdom dialogue, the accusations of incompetence agitate the Comforters even more than the accusations of injustice. A god who punishes without a good reason is scary, but a god who makes mistakes about who to punish for the right reasons is even scarier. Job consistently claims that, if he could just get a minute or two alone with God, he could clear up everything. This very formulation imagines a God who does not know what is going on in the universe that He created.

God's questions bear directly on Job's accusations of both injustice and incompetence, and they highlight Job's inability to make a convincing case for either. To call God unjust, Job would have to comprehend how all of the pieces of the universe fit together into an infinite chain of causes and effects. To call God incompetent, Job would have to understand all of the things that God does. By the end of God's cross-examination, Job, at least, understands what has happened. God has successfully defended Himself from Job's charges.

When the poem ends, the poet returns us to the world of the frame. Everything that happens after this point—the doubling of Job's fortunes, Job's new children, and his long and happy life—belongs to the tale and not the poem, so we must take them with a grain of salt. As the actual poem ends, all we know about Job is that he intends to repent—not, as the Comforters suggest, of the unknown sin that brought God's wrath upon him, but of the incorrect assumptions that lead him to become Yahweh's accuser.

God's answer to Job rejects the ideology of retributive justice in just about every way that the poet could possibly reject it. God refuses even to consider the idea that Job's suffering has anything to do with his behavior. He makes Job acknowledge that he could never understand enough to reason from a material effect back to a moral cause—even if the world did work that way. And He gives Job a brief glimpse of a universe too magnificent, too amoral, and too weird to ever work according to the principles that Job's entire culture has woven into a rigid orthodoxy more important than friendship or compassion.

But God's response goes further. The connection between morality and material circumstance is just one of the things that human beings think we understand but don't. The human perspective is not just limited; it is extraordinarily biased in favor of its narrow point of view. Perhaps the most important thing that Job learns from God is humility—not as a moral virtue, but as a frank acknowledgement of reality. Job's final words in chapter 42 show that he has acknowledged the limited nature of his perspective and, therefore, the inadequacy of his judgment. We get the most out of Job, I believe, when we develop a similar humility about our own point of view:

> I spoke without understanding
> Of things beyond me, which I did not know.
> Hear now, and I will speak;
> I will ask, and You will inform me.
> I had heard You with my ears,
> But now I see You with my eyes;
> Therefore, I recant and relent,
> Being but dust and ashes.
> (42:3–6)

As countless readers have pointed out, the Book of Job does not answer the question, "Why do bad things happen?" It does, however, tell us that humanity's most common answer to this question is wrong. Material misfortunes, the poet insists, do not trace back to moral choices in any way that human beings can evaluate. There are profound consequences to knowing this. It means that paying tithing won't always make our finances work out and that going to the temple won't ensure that our children go on missions. It tells us that some people will do everything that they are supposed to do and still experience profound tragedies while others will flout all of the laws of God and die rich, old, and in bed. It means that the universe does not belong to the category of things that we can predict or control.

Chapter Seven

"The Emancipator of Your God": Job's Critique of Religious Orthodoxy

You realize by now the part you played
To stultify the Deuteronomist
And change the tenor of religious thought.
My thanks are to you for releasing me
From moral bondage to the human race.
The only free will at first was man's,
Who could do good or evil as he chose.
I had no choice but must follow him
With forfeits and rewards he understood—
Unless I liked to suffer loss of worship.
I had to prosper good and punish evil.
You changed all that. You set me free to reign.
You are the Emancipator of your God.
　　　　　　—Robert Frost, *A Masque of Reason*

Robert Frost's 1945 verse play *A Masque of Reason* presents itself as "the 43rd chapter of Job." Set a thousand years after the action narrated in the Bible, it begins when Job and his wife happen upon a burning bush that they recognize (from William Blake's paintings) as God—whom they have not seen since the Whirlwind back in the not-so-good old days. With the perspective of a millennium, the three major players begin to talk about old times. God begins the conversation by praising Job for helping to destroy the expectation that He would always dole out rewards and punishments in exact proportion to people's moral worth. God makes it a point to thank Job for helping Him establish once and for all that "there's no connection man can reason out / Between his just deserts and what he gets."[1] And he concludes by giving Job what is perhaps the strangest and most laudatory title ever bestowed on a mere mortal by a divine being: "the Emancipator of your God." These are strong words. Like the Job poet, Frost does not hesitate to criticize, in the harshest terms possible, the idea that God must reward all good actions and punish all bad ones. Such a view places God "in moral bondage to the human race." It destroys God's agency by setting up decision rules that determine how He must interact with His own creations. If they obey a few simple commandments, He has to give them money, health, and attractive spouses; if they break the rules, He must make them suffer. Adherents of this view therefore turn the Author of the Universe into something like a cosmic Pez dispenser. God hails Job as the "Emancipator of [his] God" because the Book of Job forever removed from God the expectation that He will structure people's earthly circumstances in direct proportion to their moral worth.

Except that it didn't. Frost certainly understood that he was declaring victory prematurely on a very stubborn misconception. The Book of Job did not put to rest the idea of a God who rewards good and punishes evil. Its first readers—the Jewish exile community in Babylon after the destruction of Jerusalem in 587 B.C.—did not suddenly give up their belief in retributive divine justice. Rather, they made it the cornerstone of their faith and their culture for the next 2,000 years. Other than the Book of Job, there is very little in the Hebrew Bible that rejects, or fails to actively support, this concept of God.

The God of Rewards and Punishments survived the Babylonian captivity intact—the Book of Job notwithstanding. And it went on to become a cornerstone of Christian morality. But Christianity had a trick that the original readers of Job lacked. With their greatly expanded views of heaven and hell, Christians could solve Job's problem by deferring rewards and punishments into an afterlife of perfect justice. Under the Book of Job's original assumptions, however, this would be cheating. As we have already seen, at the time of the Babylonian exile, the Jews had only vague notions of a life beyond this one. God's justice had to manifest itself in this world, or it didn't count. A person like Job—a completely innocent man who suffers for no easily discernible reason—was not even theoretically possible under the orthodox view of his day. This is precisely why the poet had to create him.

The principle of reward and punishment that Job refutes is often referred to as the "the law of retribution," and it constitutes one of the most important unifying principles of the Hebrew Bible. Latter-day Saints

---

1. Robert Frost, *A Masque of Reason*, 261.

sometimes refer to the law of retribution as the "law of the harvest," or "as you sow, so shall you reap." Since 1980, the LDS institute manual for the Old Testament has included the following explanation of this principle from Sterling W. Sill's 1963 book, *The Law of the Harvest*:

> One of the distinguishing characteristics of our world is that it is a place of law and order, and the basic law of creation is God's fundamental law of compensation. It says that all work must be paid for, that we can no more do a good thing without sometime, in some way receiving a reward, than we can do an evil thing without suffering a penalty. In everything that we do, including the very thoughts that we think, we are subject to this interesting, undeviating eternal law. It is just as universal in its operation as are the laws of gravity, electricity, light or heat. It is never set aside, it is never suspended or restricted, and it governs in every department of human activity. Nothing is ever denied to well-directed effort and nothing is ever achieved without it.[2]

This is certainly a common view across Christian denominations—and among non-Christians and non-theists as well. It gets reinforced from both sides. People who have done well want to think that they have done well because of their inherent superiority and moral worth. At the same time, those who have not done well, or who have experienced great tragedy, want to believe that there are reasons for their suffering—and that a better understanding of those reasons will help them improve their lot. Very few people want to live in a universe where things just happen.

The author of the Book of Job, however, wants us to consider this possibility. There is a moral order to the universe, the poet suggests, and it may or may not involve divine retribution. But even if it does, human beings lack the perspective necessary to understand the delicate chain of cause and effect connecting material circumstances to moral behavior. So, while God may work on some system of rewards and punishments, human beings can never understand enough about that system to apply it in their lives or invoke it in judgment of others. There is no universal law of retribution that human beings can ever understand.

Ironically, the simplistic view of divine retribution that the Job poem opposes vigorously is often reinforced by uncritical readings of the Book of Job itself—readings that focus on the frame with little or no attention to the poem. The fact that the frame narrative ends with God doubling all of the material possessions that Job lost in the beginning has, for more than two thousand years, encouraged readers to ignore the message of the poem

---

2. *Old Testament Student Manual Genesis–2 Samuel*, 300. The original citation for the quotation is Sterling W. Sill, *The Law of the Harvest*, 11.

and conclude that God really does always reward good and punish evil—it's just that sometimes you have to wait a few years for the reward. "The restoration of Job's fortune reveals God's purpose for all faithful believers," writes one fairly typical Protestant interpreter of Job. "God blessed Job's latter end more than his beginning. He will do the same for the children of God today, those who remain committed, steadfast and hold on to their integrity. . . . Your latter will be greater than your beginning. Your faithfulness will be rewarded by God."[3]

Reading Job this way requires us to dismiss the poetic tension between the frame and the poem—to pass over the clear fissures between the two sections and see Job as a single, continuous narrative. More disturbingly, it requires us to reject the entirety of the Job poet's accomplishment. If the only difference between Deuteronomy and Job concerns the amount of time that it takes the rewards and punishments to kick in, then the poet has offered only a tiny, and ultimately inconsequential, critique of his culture's views. Unless we are willing to see the Job poem as a radical challenge to the orthodoxy of the Job frame—along with most of the rest of the Hebrew Bible—then we can spare ourselves the considerable time and attention required to read it.

More than anything else, the Job poet wants us to know that the frame tale gets its own moral wrong. By not only restoring, but doubling, Job's material wealth, the frame ends up embracing exactly the theological narrative it should be rejecting. The Job poem is the valiant attempt of a great writer—perhaps the greatest of the ancient world—to set the story straight.

"To Stultify the Deuteronomist"

It would be difficult to overstate the psychological effect of the Babylonian captivity on the Jewish people. Nearly every other people that the Babylonians conquered ended up giving up its gods and assimilating into the great Babylonian mainstream. But the Jews were different. Rather than giving up on their god, or blaming him for their exile, the people of Israel doubled down. Yahweh did not abandon them, they reasoned, they abandoned Yahweh, and the Babylonian exile was their just punishment for centuries of whoring after false gods and rejecting the true one. They knew only too well that the prophets Ezekiel and Jeremiah had told them as much. "Yahweh's power to command submission became most apparent after his people had been defeated," writes ancient historian Michael

---

3. Sylvia K. Hardin, *Job's Belief and Faithfulness Rewarded by God*, 19.

Grant. "For it was he who was now their only *real* king. In exile, then, these men and women began to see themselves in a new light, and in terms of an even more distinctive and permanent identity, than ever before."[4]

This great outpouring of Jewish nationalism and religious fervor produced, among other things, the collection of texts that Christians now refer to as the Old Testament. Many of the records that became part of the Hebrew scriptures existed before the destruction of Jerusalem, but they did not exist as a coherent volume. During and after the exile, Jewish scholars and historians set about collecting, editing, redacting, and correlating their culture's most important texts. It was a daunting task. Their records spanned centuries and included tribal myths, histories, legal documents, prophecies, and imaginative literature. Choosing which texts to include must have been a monumental undertaking itself—and once the text were chosen, working it into something resembling a coherent narrative would have required the ablest editors of the ancient world, who, fortunately, were available.

One of the most important figures in this great editorial task was the person—or more likely the school of historians over several generations—that scholars now refer to as "The Deuteronomist," or sometimes just "D." Using both extant manuscripts and oral traditions, the Deuteronomist school appears to have created seven different books in the current Old Testament: Deuteronomy, Joshua, Judges, 1 Samuel, 2 Samuel, 1 Kings, and 2 Kings. These seven books, collectively referred to as the "Deuteronomistic histories," contain a more or less complete history of Israel from the entry into Canaan to the Babylonian captivity. And like all historians, the Deuteronomist did not just relate chronological facts. He/they structured those facts into a narrative that attempted to explain the past and give meaning to the present. This narrative very quickly became the official story.

The Deuteronomist's narrative was both simple and stark: the people of Israel got what was coming to them. They abandoned God, and He reacted exactly as Moses had once told them that He would: by leaving them to be destroyed by their enemies. According to Martin Noth, the German scholar who first proposed the Deuteronomist hypothesis in 1943, the Deuteronomist discovered "that God was recognizably at work in this history, continuously meeting the accelerating moral decline with warnings and punishments, and, finally, when these proved fruitless, with

---

4. Michael Grant, *The History of Ancient Israel*, 164.

total annihilation."[5] The Deuteronomistic Yahweh is a harsh, jealous, and easily angered deity who wields immense power and demands complete fidelity. But He is also an eminently predictable force in that he follows the law of retribution scrupulously—with generous rewards to those who obey him and swift, merciless punishments to those who do not.

The Deuteronomistic history begins (logically enough) with the Book of Deuteronomy, which takes the form of three speeches that Moses is said to have given his people as they were about to take possession of the Promised Land. Moses makes it very clear to the people of Israel that they are being given this land for only as long as they remain faithful to Yahweh and refrain from worshipping other gods. Over and over again, Moses tells the people that, "If you do forget the LORD your God and follow other gods to serve them or bow down to them, I warn you this day that you shall certainly perish" (Deut. 8:19). Moses repeats this warning eleven different times during the three speeches that constitute Deuteronomy.[6]

In addition to telling the Israelites that they will be wiped out if they worship pagan gods, the Book of Deuteronomy also admonishes the People of Israel to utterly exterminate all of the other tribes inhabiting the land—lest they be tempted to intermarry with pagans and start worshipping false gods. "You shall destroy all the peoples that the LORD [Yahweh] your God delivers to you, showing them no pity" says Moses (Deut. 7:16). The idol-worshippers must be exterminated (7:2), and any Israelite who takes up with idols must be put to death (13:6–10). Incomplete genocide is not an option.

When Moses is finished speaking to his people, God takes him aside and confides that, despite his many warnings, Israel will end up worshipping false gods and getting destroyed. "They will forsake Me and break My covenant that I made with them," God tells His prophet. "Then My anger will flare up against them, and I will abandon them and hide My countenance from them . . . because of all the evil they have done in turning to other gods" (Deut. 31:16–18). Perhaps a little too conveniently, the next six books of the Deuteronomistic history essentially show Israel working out the narrative that God prophesies at the end of Deuteronomy. The Israelites take possession of Canaan, but they fail to kill all of its original inhabitants. They start intermarrying with them and adopting their gods. And despite the many warnings that God sent through His prophets, they

5. Martin Noth, *The Deuteronomistic History*, 89.
6. See Deuteronomy 6:13–15; 7:4; 7:10; 7:26; 8:19; 11:22–26; 12:30; 28:15–20; 28:64; 29:25–28; 30:13–20.

end up rejecting Him completely, leaving Him no choice but to do what He promised to do when He lead them to the Promised Land.

As chilling as this historical narrative might have seemed, it was also extremely comforting to the Jewish exiles, for it told them that Yahweh was still their god and that they could get back into his good graces by rededicating themselves to His service. If the Israelites wanted God to bless them, all they had to do was worship him properly according to the Law that Moses had delivered to them in the wilderness. The Deuteronomistic histories offered Israel a second chance to get their relationship with Yahweh right, and they were determined to take it. Whatever the state of Israelite worship might have been before, the Jewish culture forged in the fires of Babylonian captivity was more committed to its traditions and sacred texts than any people had ever been—which allowed it to survive for most of the next 2,500 years without a homeland. The Law became their country.

In both history and theology, the Deuteronomistic writers relied on a literal, this-worldly understanding of the law of retribution. Israel was justified in exterminating the pagan tribes because those tribes had sinned by worshipping false gods. God used Israel to punish them in the same way that, in 587 b.c., He used the Babylonians to punish Israel, and for essentially the same reasons. On the flip side, Israel's newfound righteousness and dedication to Yahweh would lead to their prosperity just as inexorably as their disobedience had led to their demise. Their self-flagellating pessimism about their past contained the key to their wild optimism about their future—and the primary mechanism for both was the law of retribution.

The basic Deuteronomistic formulation of God's retributive justice found its way into many of the literary works that constitute the *Kethuvim*. The other great Wisdom poets—such as the authors of the Proverbs and the "Wisdom Psalms"[7] adopt a definition of "wisdom" that codifies the law of retribution into an intellectual maxim—something like, "It is wise to obey God because, if you don't He will make you suffer." Take, for example, the text of the First Psalm, which is often taken as a preface to the entire collection:

> Happy is the man who has not followed the counsel of the wicked,
> or taken the path of sinners,
> or joined the company of the insolent;

---

7. A handful of Psalms are traditionally considered "Wisdom Psalms" because they show strong evidence of coming from the wisdom tradition that produced Job, Proverbs, and Ecclesiastes. The list of such Psalms varies from commentator to commentator, but almost always includes: 1, 37, 49, 112, and 128.

> rather, the teaching of the LORD is his delight,
> and he studies that teaching day and night.
> He is like a tree planted beside streams of water,
> which yields its fruit in season,
> whose foliage never fades,
> and whatever it produces thrives.
> Not so the wicked;
> rather, they are like chaff that wind blows away.
> Therefore the wicked will not survive judgment,
> nor will sinners, in the assembly of the righteous.
> For the LORD cherishes the way of the righteous,
> but the way of the wicked is doomed.

The Psalmist's point could not be clearer: God rewards the righteous and punishes the wicked. This is the theology of the Job frame, of the Psalms, of the Proverbs, and of nearly every other book in the Old Testament. It remains a rigid orthodoxy for many people of faith today.

Though the Book of Job is notoriously difficult to date to a specific period, scholarly consensus hold that it was either written, or substantially revised, during the time of the Babylonian Exile—probably after the Book of Deuteronomy but during the same period as much of the Deuteronomistic history.[8] The Job poet, in other words, lived among the scholars and historians who devoted their lives to producing much of the Hebrew Bible as we know it today. He observed them, listened to them, possibly argued with them in person, and incorporated their view of God and history into his own great work—as the philosophy that God dismantles in his final speech. In the actual poem Job maintains his innocence, but on several occasions he indicates that he would be very glad for God, or his friends, to tell him what he did wrong so he can repent and get it over with. "Teach me; I shall be silent," he tells his friends early in their dialogue. "Tell me where I am

---

8. Dating the Book of Job has long been a difficult problem, since the book contains so many different elements, which could have been produced at very different times. See Pope, xxxii–xl for a discussion of the difficulties. On both internal and external evidence, Alter places the text "in the fifth century or perhaps as early as the later sixth century BCE, though it is impossible to be more precise, and one cannot exclude an early fourth-century setting" (*Wisdom Books*, 5). The Jewish Study Bible concurs: "Because of the abundance of allusions to the exilic and post-exilic Isaiah chs 40–66 and the use of the Hebrew *ha-satan*, 'the Adversary,' in a manner very similar to that in which the term is employed in the postexilic Zechariah ch 3 , it is generally agreed that the book of Job was composed sometime during the period from the mid-6th century to the mid-4th century, the Persian (Achaemenid) period (539–332 BCE)."

wrong." (6:24). But Job's consistent message throughout the poem is that his own innocence calls God's justice into question. This is not a position that the Comforters can ever accept because it would mean the impossibility of God. This is the concern that Archibald MacLeish puts into Job's mouth in his twentieth-century reworking of the story, *J.B.*: "We have no choice but to be guilty / God is unthinkable if we are innocent."[9]

From the very beginning of the Wisdom dialogue, the Comforters rest nearly all of their arguments on the law of retribution. In his first speech, without intending to criticize Job, Eliphaz invokes the law as evidence that everything will turn out fine for Job in the end. "Is not your piety your confidence?" he asks, hoping that this will comfort his friend. "Where have the upright been destroyed?" (4:6–7). In the later chapters, though, Elihu comes up with what he presents as irrefutable evidence of Job's guilt—evidence that consists of nothing more than an unwavering assertion of the law of retribution:

> Therefore, men of understanding, listen to me;
> Wickedness be far from God,
> Wrongdoing, from Shaddai!
> For He pays a man according to his actions,
> And provides for him according to his conduct;
> For God surely does not act wickedly;
> Shaddai does not pervert justice.
> (34:10–12)

Job's Comforters need so badly to disprove Job's innocence that they interpolate every possible argument—even correct ones—into a narrative that proves his guilt. In his first speech, Zophar, the most confrontational of all the Comforters, comes very close to the poet's understanding of God:

> Would you discover the mystery of God?
> Would you discover the limit of the Almighty?
> Higher than heaven—what can you do?
> Deeper than Sheol—what can you know?
> Its measure is longer than the earth
> And broader than the sea.
> Should He pass by, or confine,
> Or call an assembly, who can stop Him?
> For He knows deceitful men;
> When He sees iniquity, does He not discern it?
> (11:7–11)

---

9. Archibald MacLeish, *J.B.*, 111.

Zophar gets almost everything right: God's understanding is greater than our understanding; He sees more than we can possibly see; He has a perspective that we can never inhabit. But rather than following these assumptions through to their logical conclusion—that we don't know enough to judge other people based on their material circumstances—Zophar concludes merely that Job does not know enough to say that he is innocent, for he cannot possibly understand all of the ways that God knows him to be guilty.

As readers, we do not have the option of siding with the Comforters. The frame narrative does everything that a narrative can do to take that option away from us. We know from the outset that Job is "a blameless and upright man who fears God and shuns evil" (1:8). And the narrative shows that Job is permitted to suffer, not because he does anything wrong, but because he did everything right and God wanted to prove something to Satan.

The poet has carefully structured the poem to make us confront the fact that Job is innocent and yet suffers. To read Job with integrity, we must stare this uncomfortable fact in the face from the beginning of the frame (when God assures us that Job is righteous and yet sanctions his suffering) all the way to the end of the poem (when God speaks to Job from a whirlwind without ever telling him what his misery means). The poet consistently tests, and ultimately rejects the fundamental premise of Deuteronomistic history and theology—the supposed law of divine retribution—through the elaborate thought experiment that we call the Book of Job.

"And Change the Tenor of Religious Thought"

Up to this point, I have been looking at the way that the Job poet critiques a specific orthodoxy: the law of retribution, or the belief that God always rewards righteousness and punishes disobedience in ways that we can readily understand. In this reading of the poem, Job's Comforters function allegorically, as stand-ins for the Deuteronomistic historians and the cultural values that they were in the process of creating during the Job poet's life. But we can also read the Book of Job as a critique of all rigid orthodoxies—and of the way that holding too tightly to any abstract ideology destroys our ability to relate to other human beings. To read Job this way, we must shift our perspectives slightly and see Job's Comforters, not merely as allegories of a culture, but also as scared human beings who fail miserably in their attempt to comfort a friend.

The frame tale introduces Eliphaz, Bildad, and Zophar as Job's closest friends who set out to console him at some sacrifice to their own affairs. In the frame, they do nothing but listen to Job for seven days without saying a word (a pretty good strategy, actually). But the frame's Comforters do not need to contradict Job, who merely accepts his suffering cheerfully and praises the Lord. In the poem, though, the Comforters become Job's tormentors because his very existence represents a profound challenge to their understanding of the universe. If they cannot seize control of his narrative, they will have to radically refashion their understanding of the universe. The moment that Job declares his innocence, he questions God's judgment—and his friends must choose between their friendship and their religious orthodoxy.

The Comforters choose orthodoxy. We are right to be a little bit surprised by this. They have travelled long distances to comfort their close friend, who has just lost all ten of his children and now suffers from running sores on every inch of his body. Even in the ancient world, such a man would have had a strong claim to the compassion of total strangers. For his best friends to refuse him any human kindness would have seemed nearly as perverse to Job's original readers as it does to us. Job says as much himself the first time he responds to their criticisms:

> A friend owes loyalty to one who fails,
> Though he forsakes the fear of the Almighty;
> My comrades are fickle, like a wadi,
> Like a bed on which streams once ran.
> They are dark with ice;
> Snow obscures them;
> But when they thaw, they vanish;
> In the heat, they disappear where they are.
> Their course twists and turns;
> They run into the desert and perish
>
> . . .
>
> Do you devise words of reproof,
> But count a hopeless man's words as wind?
> You would even cast lots over an orphan,
> Or barter away your friend.
> (6:14–28)

But Job's pleading falls on deaf ears. He begs his friends to "be so good as to face me" (6:28)—to look in his eyes and acknowledge his humanness and his suffering—but they do not. Rather, they persist in offering abstract arguments about Job and God. No man can truly claim to be innocent, they insist, for no creature can be "cleared by his Maker" (4:17). God's ways are not man's ways, and we are not meant to understand God's mysteries (11:7). Mortals, who are no more than maggots and worms, cannot presume to judge the greatness of God (25:6). The more that Job presses his claim to human compassion, the more abstract their arguments become until, in the end, Job ceases to be a human being who needs comfort and becomes simply a theological problem that needs a solution.

The actions of the Comforters, of course, are shaped by a Deuteronomistic theology that goes to great length to force people to choose orthodoxy over personal relationships. This is why the Mosaic Law requires that blasphemers and idol worshippers be put to death by those who love them the most (Deut. 13:6, 9). Under the Law, with its jealous and demanding god, all bonds of family and friendship must be sacrificed to ideology when a conflict between them occurs. One's relationship to God is entirely separate from, and more important than, one's relationship with other human beings.

This aspect of Deuteronomistic religion would eventually become the focus of the intense critique that we now call the Sermon on the Mount. There and elsewhere, Jesus argued that we cannot separate our relationship with other people from our relationship with God. Human beings matter, even if they are women taken in adultery, or prodigal sons, or members of foreign tribes—all of whom, according to the Deuteronomist, had to be put to death. Jesus begged to differ: "And the King shall answer and say unto them, Verily I say unto you, Inasmuch as ye have done it unto one of the least of these my brethren, ye have done it unto me" (Matt. 25:40). This was perhaps the most important theme of Christ's earthly ministry.

But loving others as we love ourselves is a divine principle not a human one; Christ calls us to transcend human nature, while the Deuteronomist asks us only to succumb to it. By turning on Job and attacking him for refusing to acknowledge his sins, the Comforters react in a very human way to a set of facts that threatens to disrupt their worldview. None of us wants to reject our core assumptions about the universe and start all over again. It is hard work, and it deprives us of nearly everything that makes us feel secure. But the unconditional love that Christ requires of us cannot coexist with any ideology that requires us to reject those who do not hold it.

One need not be religious to destroy a relationship by protecting an ideology at the expense of a friend. To read Job correctly, I believe, we must read ourselves into the role of the Comforters by asking what plain evidence we may be aggressively dismissing—and what human relationships we might be actively destroying—in order to remain possessed of our comfortable ideological narratives. Such questions can be dangerous to religious orthodoxies, whose primary function is to provide comforting, and comfortable, narratives. But the comfortableness of a religious orthodoxy exists in direct proportion to its rigidity, as people will always go to drastic lengths to preserve what gives them comfort.

The Job poet ultimately insists that being a good friend is more important than holding firmly to a religious orthodoxy—and this, I believe, is the poem's most consequential critique of the Deuteronomist. Deuteronomy tells us that we must reject (often by stoning them to death) friends and family members who stray from the faith. It leaves no room for loving people when we think they are wrong. When Job's remonstrations cross the line into theological incorrectness, therefore, his friends withdraw their friendship, causing one of Job's saddest laments:

> If you were in my place;
> I would barrage you with words,
> I would wag my head over you.
> I would encourage you with words,
> My moving lips would bring relief.
> If I speak, my pain will not be relieved,
> And if I do not—what have I lost?
> Now He has truly worn me out;
> You have destroyed my whole community.
> (16:4–7)

It is for their failure as friends, I believe, and not for their inadequacy as theologians, that God finally rebukes the Comforters.

The Job poet dared to critique, and dismantle, the most powerful religious orthodoxy of his culture by confronting it with a set of facts that it could not accommodate. But beyond refuting this one particular orthodoxy, the poet demonstrated for us in excruciating detail how rigid orthodoxies of any kind can cause us to renounce both overwhelming evidence and basic human decency before abandoning our most cherished beliefs. The most profound readings of Job, I believe, recognize that the great poem is not just about suffering, or retribution, or God, or Satan, or knowing that Redeemers live; it is about how rigid orthodoxies can destroy our relationships and, thereby, our humanity.

Chapter Eight

Anticipating Christianity: Why Job's Redeemer Does Not Live—and How He Does

I know that my Redeemer lives.
What comfort this sweet sentence gives!
He lives, he lives, who once was dead.
He lives, my ever-living Head.
He lives to bless me with his love.
He lives to plead for me above.
He lives my hungry soul to feed.
He lives to bless in time of need.
— "I Know that My Redeemer Lives,"
LDS Hymnal #136

What Comfort This Sweet Sentence Gives

Before I ever read the Book of Job, I could sing all four verses of "I Know that My Redeemer Lives" by heart. I could even sort of play it on the piano and did frequently in the small Spanish branches that I served in while on my mission. "I Know that My Redeemer Lives" has been one of the "regulars" in every ward that I have ever been a part of, and I suspect that most active Latter-day Saints sing it many times every year.

When I began attending Catholic masses at the university where I currently work, I discovered that Mormons are not the only ones who sing this hymn. With somewhat different words and completely different music, "I Know that My Redeemer Lives" can be found in Catholic hymnals too. Lutherans, Methodists, Baptists, Presbyterians, Mennonites, Nazarenes, Handel's *Messiah*—pretty much everybody sings one of several different hymns based on the famous lines from Job 19:25, which the King James

Bible renders, "for I know that my redeemer liveth, and that he shall stand at the latter day upon the earth." It is therefore with great trepidation—knowing that I risk the wrath of an ecumenical army of choir directors—that I must insist that Job's redeemer does not and cannot live.

The case for a Messianic reading of Job 19:25, I will suggest, has been dramatically overstated by Christians for nearly two thousand years—and this overstatement found its way into the King James Bible in ways that probably made a Christological reading inevitable. But we must be careful. If we acknowledge that Job has a living "redeemer"—in the context that Job uses the word—then we must also agree that he has been falsely accused and inappropriately punished—as, in Job's world, that is the sort of problem that "redeemers" solved.

The Hebrew word that the King James Bible translates as "redeemer" is *go'el*, a form of the fairly common biblical word *ga'al*, which refers to a specific kinship function in Ancient Israel. The *ga'al* was the closest male relative of a deceased man and was charged with protecting the decedent's reputation, honor, or property in pretty much any way that these things needed protecting. In his commentary on Job, Marvin Pope writes that a *ga'al* was "obliged to exact vengeance in a blood feud (Deut. 19:6–12; 2 Sam. 14:11) or otherwise look after the interests of his kinsman by redeeming him from slavery (Lev. 25:48) or regaining the family property (Lev. 25:25), including the decedent's widow in order to provide him an heir by proxy."[1]

Other translations of Job 19:25 render *go'el* as "avenger," "defender," or "vindicator." And other passages of the King James Bible translate *ga'al* (and related words) as "revenger of blood" (Num. 35:19; 2 Sam. 14:11), "avenger" (Deut. 19:12; Josh. 20:3), and "kinsman" (Num. 5:8; Ruth 3:9). All of these translations capture part, but only part, of the Hebrew *ga'al*'s responsibilities. A better, though much more ironic, translation would be "fixer"—in the way that it is used by some of the more unsavory characters in the gangster movies of the 1930s and 1940s. The *ga'al* fixed whatever needed fixing after a man died—up to, and including, marrying his wife and siring children in his name.

The most famous *ga'al* story in the Bible is the Book of Ruth. When Ruth's husband, Mahlon, dies, she proclaims herself a follower of Yahweh and returns to Israel with her mother-in-law, Naomi. There they make a connection with Boaz, Mahlon's kinsman, who allows Ruth to glean barley in his fields. After some prodding by Ruth and Naomi, Boaz agrees

---

1. Marvin H. Pope, *Anchor Bible: Job*, 146.

to marry Ruth and become her husband's "redeemer." Before he can do so, however, he must arrange for a closer relative—whose claim to the role of *gaʾal* outweighs his own—to forfeit that right:

> Then [Boaz] took ten elders of the town and said, "Be seated here"; and they sat down. He said to the redeemer, "Naomi, now returned from the country of Moab, must sell the piece of land which belonged to our kinsman Elimelech. I thought I should disclose the matter to you and say: Acquire it in the presence of those seated here and in the presence of the elders of my people. If you are willing to redeem it, redeem! But if you will not redeem, tell me, that I may know. For there is no one to redeem but you, and I come after you." "I am willing to redeem it," he replied. Boaz continued, "When you acquire the property from Naomi and from Ruth the Moabite, you must also acquire the wife of the deceased, so as to perpetuate the name of the deceased upon his estate." The redeemer replied, "Then I cannot redeem it for myself, lest I impair my own estate. You take over my right of redemption, for I am unable to exercise it." (Ruth 4:2–6)

In Ruth, as elsewhere in the Hebrew scriptures, the *gaʾal* relationship conveys both rights and responsibilities that can plausibly be translated as "redeeming" in much the same way that one "redeems" an item from a pawn shop. Does this mean that a *gaʾal* figure could not refer to Christ or the coming Messiah—or that this sort of "redemption" could not refer to the Atonement? Of course not. The Hebrew Bible describes Yahweh as a *gaʾal* in several places (Ex. 6:6, Jer. 1:34), and the *gaʾal* relationship makes perfect sense as a symbol for both the Hebrew Messiah and the Christian Jesus Christ. There are many scenarios in which an Old Testament figure might plausibly talk about the prophesied Messiah as a *gaʾal*. But Job 19:25 is not one of them, as a fuller reading of the chapter demonstrates:

> Know that God has wronged me;
> He has thrown up siege works around me.
> I cry, "Violence!" but am not answered;
> I shout, but can get no justice.
> He has barred my way; I cannot pass;
> He has laid darkness upon my path.
> He has stripped me of my glory,
> Removed the crown from my head.
> He tears down every part of me; I perish;
> He uproots my hope like a tree.
>
> 　　. . .
>
> He alienated my kin from me;
> My acquaintances disown me.

My relatives are gone;
My friends have forgotten me.
My dependents and maidservants regard me as a stranger;
I am an outsider to them.

                    ...

All my bosom friends detest me;
Those I love have turned against me.
My bones stick to my skin and flesh;
I escape with the skin of my teeth.
Pity me, pity me! You are my friends;
For the hand of God has struck me!
Why do you pursue me like God,
Maligning me insatiably?
O that my words were written down;
Would they were inscribed in a record,
Incised on a rock forever
With iron stylus and lead!
But I know that my Vindicator lives;
In the end He will testify on earth.
(19:6–10; 13–15; 19–25)

When we read the chapter in context, we see Job building the case that God has deprived him of both reputation and property—both things that, according to Hebrew custom, require the posthumous services of a *ga'al*. But when he goes through his kinship network, he acknowledges that God's persecution has alienated him from (or outright killed) all of the close relatives who would normally perform such a role. Job is not looking for someone to redeem him from his sinful human nature or from spiritual bondage. He wants somebody to testify on his behalf to convince God that he did not do whatever God thinks he did—and therefore to restore, if only posthumously, both his reputation and his estate.

The standard Christian interpretation of the last two lines makes little sense in this context. It requires us to believe that Job, in the middle of criticizing God's justice and reprimanding his friends for their lack of compassion, felt suddenly inspired to prophesy of a coming Messiah (who, as a non-Jew, he did not believe in) who would one day make it possible for him to repent of his sins (which he refuses to do because he does not think he has any sins to repent of) and have eternal life (which was not even a thing when Job was written). And not only that, Job also speaks of the Messiah as though he has already been born, lived, died, and been resurrected—just so that Christians will one day be able to quote him in songs about the Resurrection.

A much more likely scenario is that Christians have been misreading this verse for two thousand years because we have always felt compelled to find allusions to Christ in the Old Testament. The King James scholars felt the same way, and they translated this verse—not entirely accurately—in a way that virtually guaranteed that future generations would read Christ into it. And as knowledge of the original context fades, and more and more people treat the Bible as 30,000 loosely related proof texts for whatever they happen to believe, the line "I know that my redeemer lives" has become irrefutable proof of Job's Messianic worldview. It hardly seems to matter that, to agree with Job on this point, we must grant all of Satan's arguments in the book and reject all of God's.

Christ in the Old Testament

The Book that Christians call "the Bible" consists of two very different collections of documents: thirty-nine Hebrew texts written before, or shortly after the Babylonian Captivity, and twenty-seven Greek texts written during the first century after Christ. When we call the first collection "the Old Testament," and the second "the New Testament," we are saying that both collections have the same essential purpose and that both give a testimony of the same thing—namely, the divine nature of Jesus Christ.

Nearly all Christians believe this, of course. Anyone who accepts the Jesus of the New Testament must also accept the authority of the Old Testament—for the simple reason that much of the New Testament was written to convince first-century Jews that Jesus was the Messiah foreseen by the Hebrew prophets. The Greek word *christós*, or "anointed one," is simply the best translation the New Testament writers had for the Hebrew word *messiah*. "Jesus Christ" is not so much a name as it is an argument: the assertion that the Galilean teacher named Yeshua was the long-anticipated Messiah of Hebrew scripture.

To make this case, New Testament writers immersed themselves in the Hebrew scriptures to pull out everything that could be known about the Messiah of prophecy. Some common aspects of Messiahship were clearly perceived by the Jews of the first century: he would be born in Bethlehem (Micah 5:2), his mother would be a virgin (Isa. 7:14), and he absolutely, positively had to be a descendent of King David (2 Sam. 7:12–13; Isa. 9:7; Eze. 37:24–25). This is why the Gospel of Matthew—the New Testament book most concerned with establishing Jesus as the Messiah—opens with a complete genealogy of the generations from David to Jesus, establishing the latter's right (albeit through an acknowledged stepfather) to occupy the Davidic throne.

But the early Christians went well beyond the Hebrew scriptures normally cited in discussions of the Messiah in order to make their case. The author of Matthew reads passages as Messianic prophecies that had never been strongly considered before, such as Hosea 11:1 (which says that God called his son out of Egypt) and Zechariah 11:12–13 (which speaks of somebody being betrayed and sold for thirty pieces of silver). The Gospel of Matthew includes dozens of references back to Old Testament statements, and the author marks many of them clearly as fulfillments of prophecy.

The New Testament introduces another way of connecting Jesus to the Old Testament that would become very common in the early Christian communities: a connection strategy called "typology." A "type" is an allusion to something that has not happened yet—an action or plot element that predicts something that will happen in the future. For example, the New Testament story of Herod's "Massacre of the Innocents" (Matt. 2:16–18) contains easily identifiable parallels to the story of the Pharaoh's massacre of male Hebrew children in Exodus 1:15–22. Nothing in Matthew suggests that Herod killed Jewish children to allude back to the days of Moses. The text suggests something far more audacious: Pharaoh's massacre prefigured Herod's in order to demonstrate to all the ages that Moses was a type of Christ.

From a very early date, then, Christian interpretation has emphasized typological connections between the Old and the New Testaments. Abraham's binding of Isaac was a type of God's sacrifice of his only son; Moses leading the Children of Israel out of Egypt became a type of Christ's Atonement leading us from the bondage of sin; Jonah spending three days in the belly of the whale was seen as a type of Christ rising after three days in the grave. Christians have long read all of these connections (and many more) as predictive symbols that God used to prepare people for the life and ministry of Jesus Christ.[2]

Like nearly every sympathetic figure in the Old Testament, Job would come to be read as a type of Jesus Christ—and specifically as one whose unmerited suffering prefigured the sinless Christ's atoning sacrifice. These typological connections would become the basis of one of the most im-

---

2. I take up these typological connections at some length in an earlier book, *New Testaments: Cognition, Closure, and the Figural Logic of the Sequel,* 17–38.

portant works of theology of the early middle ages: the six-volume *Morals of Job* by Pope Gregory the Great, published soon after his elevation to the papacy in 590. For Gregory, Job is the perfect symbol for the suffering Christ, both because he shares that suffering and because he foresees how it will lead to a triumphant resurrection:

> For he says, *For I know that my Redeemer liveth*. As if he said in express terms; "The unbelievers may know that He was scourged, mocked, struck with the palms of the hand, covered with a crown of thorns, besmeared with spittings, crucified, dead: I, with sure faith, believe Him to live after death; I confess with unreserved voice, 'that my Redeemer liveth,' Who died by the hands of wicked men." And how, O blessed Job, through His Resurrection, thou trustest to the resurrection of thine own flesh.[3]

Gregory's treatise, Mark Larrimore surmises, "interwove the rest of the Christian scriptures so tightly with Job that *Morals in Job* became the go-to book for anyone seeking to understand the nature of existence in this middle region of sin and suffering."[4]

Gregory's understanding of Job was probably inevitable, given the way that he and all other Medieval Christians encountered the text. Once the poem called Job was bound with other books and presented as part of a larger text, there was no way for most people to read it any other way. As Larrimore aptly points out, Job has been part of something else for nearly all of its history as a book.[5] Scholarly exegesis of Job as a stand-alone text is less than a century old. Jews have read it as part of the *Kethuvim* and the *Tanakh* for thousands of years, and Christians have regarded it as part of the Old Testament and the Bible for nearly as long. Nearly everybody who read Job before the twentieth century came to the text already considering it a chapter in a coherent larger story.

We can never know the motivations or assumptions of the poet who wrote the Book of Job. We can guess, but we do not know how this brilliant artist fit into the Jewish community that compiled and edited the Hebrew Bible in the aftermath of the Babylonian captivity. Nor can we ever know for sure how Job was read and understood by early generations of Christians, though we know that they were familiar with some version of the story and spoke approvingly of Job's patience (James 5:11). But we do know that Job has been an integral part of the Christian scriptures for thousands of years and that generations of Christians have found mean-

---

3. Gregory the Great, *Morals on the Book of Job*, vol. 2, 161–62.
4. Mark Larrimore, *The Book of Job: A Biography*, 68.
5. Ibid., 27.

ing and inspiration in its words. It is now a constitutive element of the Christian tradition, which means that Christians have a responsibility to understand how it fits into our belief system.

To do so, however, we have to do more than just isolate a few passages out of context and turn them into typological proof texts. When we emphasize phrases like "I know that my redeemer lives"—which rely on the accidents of translation and actively resist contextual explication—we forge very weak connections to the New Testament. We can do much better. Job is one of the easiest books in the Hebrew Bible to fit into a Christian worldview. Its ethical structures, its expansive cosmology, and its disdain for Deuteronomistic legalism all fit comfortably with the New Testament message. And this is true whether or not Job's redeemer actually lives.

Finding Christ in the Book of Job

As I have suggested, some ways of connecting the Old and New Testaments together are stronger than others. Weak connections usually depend on a single word or a fleeting image. Such connections insist, often on very scanty evidence, that Old Testament figures understood and actively thought about Christ—and even lived their lives as anticipatory symbols of His divine mission. These connections are weak because they operate only at the surface of the two texts; they are not particularly helpful either. Knowing that Jonah spent three days in the belly of a fish in order to create a living prophecy of Christ's death and resurrection doesn't really tell us anything useful about either Christ or Jonah—or even about the number three.

To forge strong connections between the Old and New Testaments, we need to work harder than most of us really want to work. We need to understand that the record of God's dealings with a semi-nomadic iron-age society will contain a lot of stuff that will not make sense to us. When we try too hard to make everything fit nicely, we end up sounding remarkably silly. Jacob and his sons did not have Family Home Evening, and Job's Comforters were not home teachers. Much of the Old Testament is as irreducibly strange to us as an episode of *Real Housewives* would have been to Moses.

But some of it is not. Hebrew culture contained wisdom, spirituality, and great beauty—much of which found its way into both the New Testament and the modern world through the books of the Hebrew Bible.

We need not see every word of the Old Testament as a cryptic prediction of Christ in order to appreciate the very real connections between the Ancient Hebrews and the early Christians (most of who were slightly less Ancient Hebrews themselves). Many of the ideas that gave Christianity its great vitality had been worked hundreds of years before Christ by the poets and prophets of the Hebrew Bible.

In the rest of this chapter, I will examine some of the elements of Job that anticipate the New Testament and the Christian message much more powerfully than the isolated verses that usually get read as types and prophecies. These strong connections, I argue, get to the heart of what we mean when we say that Job is a "Christian text"—not that it spells out "Jesus Christ" if you hold it up to the light just right, but that its theology, its cosmological assumptions, and its moral vision are recognizably Christian in important ways.

Job Is a Universal Story

Job is a Hebrew poem about an extremely sympathetic non-Hebrew character—one described by God himself as "a blameless and upright man who fears God and shuns evil!" This is no small matter given the Old Testament's emphasis on nation and covenant. And Job is not just incidentally non-Jewish; he is aggressively non-Jewish in ways that we are clearly supposed to notice. The poet avoids using Jewish names for any of the characters in the original dialogue, and he steers away from place names connected to the Israelite nations. From this alone, we might conclude that the Job poet saw non-Israelites very differently than the Deuteronomist did—not as enemies to be killed, or even as threats to be avoided, but as fully equal children of God.

The universalizing ethic of Job becomes unmistakable when we look at the names that the various characters use for God. In the frame tale, the narrator uses the Hebrew tetragram YHWH, or Yahweh. But as soon as the poem begins, Job and his Comforters use generic, non-Jewish names for God, such as El and Shaddai.[6] But when God himself shows up at the end of the poem, the narrator once again calls Him Yahweh—the God of Israel—and He talks directly to Job as he once talked to Moses. This fact has profound theological implications, as it strongly suggests, at least for the poet, that Yahweh is a universal God who treats the people of all

---

6. For a parsing of the names of God used in Job, see Pope, *Anchor Bible: Job*, xxiii–xxiv.

tribes the same. What a remarkable notion this must have been to people familiar with the "God of Israel" portrayed in ultra-nationalistic books that we now call Deuteronomy and Joshua.

The Book of Job suggests that a part of the Jewish tradition has long seen God as a universal deity. The tension between this notion of God and its opposite—that the Jews have a special relationship with Yahweh that others can never have—persists well into the New Testament. John the Baptist occasionally spoke against the latter view. "Think not to say within yourselves, we have Abraham to *our* father," he once told a group of assembled Jews. "For I say unto you, that God is able of these stones to raise up children unto Abraham" (Matt. 3:9). But the tension persisted throughout the Christian movement until it almost tore the early Church apart—a history that forms the central conflict of the Book of Acts.

A major question for the first generation of Jesus's followers was "Are we Jews or are we Christians?" This question erupts periodically throughout Acts in controversies over things like circumcision and the eating of food offered to idols (Acts 15). But a central question of the Book of Acts—"Are Christ's teachings for the Jews alone or for all of humanity?"—was answered rather spectacularly in Acts 10 with a vision to the Apostle Peter shortly before he meets the Roman Centurion Cornelius, a gentile who had been prepared by God to receive the Gospel. The Bible tells us that Peter:

> fell into a trance. And saw heaven opened, and a certain vessel descending unto him, as it had been a great sheet knit at the four corners, and let down to the earth: Wherein were all manner of fourfooted beasts of the earth, and wild beasts, and creeping things, and fowls of the air. And there came a voice to him, Rise, Peter; kill, and eat. But Peter said, Not so, Lord; for I have never eaten any thing that is common or unclean. And the voice *spake* unto him again the second time, What God hath cleansed, *that* call not thou common. (Acts 10:10–15)

Peter is shaken by the vision, much as a modern Latter-day Saint might be shaken by a vision in which God commands her to smoke cigarettes and drink gin. But Peter immediately understands what God is trying to tell him. When he is finally summoned to meet Cornelius, he explains that "it is an unlawful thing for a man that is a Jew to keep company, or come unto one of another nation; but God hath shewed me that I should not call any man common or unclean" (Acts 10:28). And when the meeting concludes, Peter, who had an important lesson to learn that day, "opened his mouth, and said, "Of a truth I perceive that God is no respecter of persons: But in every nation he that feareth him, and worketh righteousness, is accepted with him" (vv. 34–35). One suspects that he might have been less surprised if he had read the Book of Job more carefully.

Job Defines Morality as a Way of Treating Other People

As reported in the New Testament, Jesus Christ had a tricky relationship with the Law of Moses. "Think not that I came to destroy the law or the prophets," he says in the Sermon on the Mount. "I came not to destroy, but to fulfill" (Matt. 5:17–18). But he frequently expresses contempt for those who try to use the Law as a substitute for personal righteousness. He had little patience for strict rules of Sabbath observance (Matt. 12:1–14), ritual cleansing (Matt. 15:1–3), or with the idea that technically obeying the law was the same thing as righteousness (Matt. 5:21–44). When the scribes and Pharisees challenge the disciples for eating while ritually unclean, Jesus gives them a lesson on the difference between holiness and legalistic obedience:

> Do not ye yet understand, that whatsoever entereth in at the mouth goeth into the belly, and is cast out into the draught? But those things which proceed out of the mouth come forth from the heart; and they defile the man. For out of the heart proceed evil thoughts, murders, adulteries, fornications, thefts, false witness, blasphemies: These are the things which defile a man: but to eat with unwashen hands defileth not a man. (Matt. 15:17–20)

Jesus is also fairly specific about what constitutes holy behavior, and mostly it involves other people. Love your enemies, turn the other cheek, forgive people—that sort of thing. These other-directed moral imperatives have always defined Christianity, but they are by no means unique to Jesus Christ, who always gave credit to the Jewish tradition for the ethical code he taught to his followers. Consider a famous passage in Matthew in which Jesus is tempted by a lawyer to name the greatest commandment in the law:

> Jesus said unto him, Thou shalt love the Lord thy God with all thy heart, and with all thy soul, and with all thy mind. This is the first and great commandment. And the second is like unto it, Thou shalt love thy neighbour as thyself. On these two commandments hang all the law and the prophets. (Matt. 22:37–40)

Jesus isn't making this up as he goes along. He is dutifully quoting the Torah. The first commandment comes from Deuteronomy 6:5, and the second from Leviticus 19:18. From His perspective, loving your neighbor as you love yourself has always been a part of the Jewish tradition—just a part that often got lost in the ritual observances that Jesus considered much less important.

The Job poet thought much the same way. As a non-Israelite, of course, Job was free from many ritual obligations—which may very well have been the author's point in making him a non-Israelite. When he and his Comforters speak of "righteousness," they almost always refer to the treatment of other people. For example, when Eliphaz finally turns against Job for good he tells him, "You have sent away widows empty-handed; / The strength of the fatherless is broken" (22:9). When Job lists his virtues in his final speech, he says nothing about praying, fasting, or physically worshipping God in any way. Rather, he talks about how he has treated other people:

> Did I deny the poor their needs,
> Or let a widow pine away,
> By eating my food alone,
> The fatherless not eating of it also?
> Why, from my youth he grew up with me as though I were his father;
> Since I left my mother's womb I was her guide.
> I never saw an unclad wretch,
> A needy man without clothing,
> Whose loins did not bless me
> As he warmed himself with the shearings of my sheep.
> (31:16–20)

Job, his friends, and the author of the poem simply take it for granted that "virtue" is best seen as a measure of how well we treat other people. The author has no desire to start a fan club for Yahweh. The poem says nothing about praying, sacrificing animals, or singing psalms of praise. It doesn't even say anything about refraining from idol worship—the go-to definition of morality in the culture that produced Job. This is one of the more relevant connections between Job and the New Testament. "Pure religion" in the Book of Job means something very similar to what it means in the Book of James: "to visit the fatherless and widows in their affliction, and to keep [oneself] unspotted from the world" (James 1:27).

Job Calls Us to Be Good Samaritans

When they encounter a friend in spiritual and physical agony, Job's Comforters tell him that he should pray, look on the bright side, and keep the commandments. Most importantly, though, they tell him that he should never, ever question the goodness of God. In other words, they give Job all of the official, culturally sanctioned answers to his profound and culturally inconvenient questions. From some perspectives, this would mean that Job's Comforters do everything right—but not from the perspective of our poet, who suggests that they miss the whole point of their duty to "mourn with those who mourn and comfort those who stand in need of comfort" (Mosiah 18:9). To be a comforter, one must comfort.

Christ, too, expounded on the difference between doing one's religious duty and comforting those who stand in need of comfort. In the parable of the Good Samaritan (Luke 10:25–27), both a priest and a Levite pass by the man who had been left for dead—almost certainly because contact with a dead person would have made them ritually unclean. From a moral perspective based on ritual, then, they were absolutely correct to avoid the possibility of contamination. The whole point of the parable, though, is to push us to a higher ethical understanding—the understanding of the Samaritan (also ritually unclean) who ministers to the fallen man whose own religious leaders would not.

Job's Comforters have much in common with the priest and the Levite. They react most negatively when Job accuses God of being unjust—an almost unimaginable blasphemy from the perspective of their culture, and they do not want to be contaminated by Job's sinful speech. After Job appears to criticize God in a response to Eliphaz, the first words out of Bildad's mouth are "how long will you speak such things?" (8:2). Soon after, Zophar exclaims, "you may mock without being rebuked . . . but would that God might speak / And talk to you Himself" (11:3–5). And in his second speech Eliphaz asks,

> Are God's consolations not enough for you,
> And His gentle words to you?
> How your heart has carried you away,
> How your eyes have failed you,
> That you could vent your anger on God,
> And let such words out of your mouth!
> (15:11–13)

One of the reasons that the Comforters speak so harshly to Job, then, is that they feel a religious duty to contradict his blasphemous criticisms of God. The frame narrative makes much of the fact that Job "said nothing sinful" (2:10). Religious commentators often read this into the poem and insist that Job never actually crosses the line into blasphemy. But let's not kid ourselves. Swearing an oath, as Job does, "by the God who has deprived me of justice" (27:2) would have been considered blasphemous by almost any Jewish audience in the ancient world. It would not go over well in many Christian congregations today.

When Job says things like this, he forces his interlocutors to choose between supporting their friend and supporting their God. Simply being in the presence of a blasphemous utterance had moral consequences for pious Jews. Jewish law took blasphemy very seriously. Blasphemers had to be stoned, and those who heard the blasphemy had to do the stoning (Lev. 24:13–14). Job's Comforters are not Jewish, of course, but they are literary characters created for a Jewish audience who would have immediately appreciated their moral dilemma: to sympathize with Job as he criticized God would have made them complicit in his blasphemy. To remain free of sin, they had to abandon a friend in a time of great need.

Much like the priest and the Levite in the parable of the Good Samaritan, Job's Comforters fear being contaminated by something theologically objectionable. The priest and the Levite do not want to risk ritual uncleanliness by touching a dead body. Eliphaz, Bildad, and Zophar don't want to risk the moral contagion of listening to Job's blasphemous complaints against God. In both cases, the representatives of the orthodox religion choose abstract theological purity above the physical and spiritual needs of another human being. For both Jesus and the Job poet, it is the wrong choice.

Job Illustrates the Need for Reconciliation between God and Humanity

If there is one uncontestable theme in the Book of Job it is that God lies entirely outside of human understanding. Job acknowledges this from the very beginning, and each of the Comforters makes it part of his argument. Elihu, too, builds most of his speeches around the fact that God's ways cannot be known, and even the Hymn to Wisdom makes this the focus of its third and final strophe. If anybody manages to read all the way to the end of Job without getting the point, Yahweh himself shouts it from a whirlwind for the last four chapters. God is not the sort of being that humans can even begin to understand.

The problem with perspective goes both ways. Human beings cannot understand God, but, at the same time, Job's God shows little ability to sympathize with human beings. God's speeches are not even as comforting as those of Job's friends. He shows no interest in Job's feelings or his pain. He sees some people making theological arguments based on false premises and decides to spend a few hours shouting sarcastic comments out of a whirlwind in order to set them straight. The Book of Job, therefore, shows us two perspectives—human and divine—that cannot be reconciled to each other. Job, therefore, introduces the argument that human beings have a desperate need for reconciliation with God, which is also a central theme of the New Testament.

As one who was both fully human and fully divine, Jesus Christ could inhabit both perspectives at the same time. He could simultaneously experience both Job's agony and God's responsibility. As Paul writes in his first epistle to Timothy, "there is one God, and one mediator between God and men, the man Christ Jesus" (1 Tim. 2:5). Only Christ can mediate between human and divine nature. Through His ministry, he made God comprehensible to human beings by speaking in parables and aphorisms—much more user-friendly forms of instruction than burning bushes and occasional shouts from whirlwinds. Thus, through His Atonement, he made human beings acceptable to God.

The Book of Job, then, sets up and defines the problem that the narrative of the New Testament attempts to solve. Like much of the Old Testament, Job shows us a God who has experiences, emotions, perspectives, and motivations we can never hope to understand. But unlike most of his contemporaries, the Job poet faces the implication of such a God head on. We cannot use our human reason to determine what God will do, nor can we use our human notions of morality to determine what God should do. The poet shows us that we can do nothing to reconcile human and divine nature. Only God can accomplish such a reconciliation—and the only way He can do so is to become human Himself.

Becoming human is how Job's Redeemer does live after all. It has nothing to do with the *ga'al* that he wishes for in chapter 19. Job does not need a witness to clear his name or an avenger to redeem his reputation. He needs, as we all need, a way to reconcile the flawed, broken, incomplete perspective of human beings with the awesome, perfect, but impossibly distant perspective of the Creator of the Universe. Christ combines these two perspectives into a single point of view—a point of view that makes it possible for human beings to have an actual relationship with God. He made it possible for us to understand God, and he made it possible for God to accept us.

Chapter Nine

Job after Auschwitz:
Refashioning Theodicy in the
Twentieth Century

What is the meaning of the suffering of innocents? Does it not prove
a world without God, an earth on which man is the only measure of
good and evil? The simplest and most common reaction would be to
decide for atheism. This would also be the reasonable reaction of all
those whose idea of God until that point was of some kindergarten
deity who distributed prizes, applied penalties, or forgave faults and
in His goodness treated men as eternal children.
　　—Emmanuel Levinas, *on "Yosl Rakover Talks to God"*

He is responsible or He is not. If He is, let us judge Him; if He is
not, let Him stop judging us.
　　—Elie Wiesel, *The Trial of God*

The Problem of Evil

In 1978, a forty-three-year old Rabbi named Harold Kushner published his first book. A year earlier, Kushner's fourteen-year-old son died
of a rare genetic disease. As he explains in his introduction, he turned to
writing both to give some structure to his own suffering and to "distill
some blessing out of Aaron's pain and tears" by helping other people with
similar struggles.[1] His book, *When Bad Things Happen to Good People* went
on to sell more than four million copies, and its title became my generation's entry point into a very old philosophical conversation known as "the
problem of evil."

---

1. Harold Kushner, *When Bad Things Happen to Good People*, 4.

In philosophical terms, we can describe *When Bad Things Happen to Good People* as a "theodicy," or an attempt to address the problem of evil by explaining how suffering and tragedy and pain can exist in a world ruled by an all-powerful and perfectly benevolent deity. If God is good, the argument goes, then He must not want evil. And if He is all-powerful, He must be able to prevent it. So the existence of evil demonstrates that God is either not entirely good or not completely powerful. In his Job-inspired play *J.B.*, Archibald MacLeish renders this as a memorable quatrain:

> I heard upon his dry dung heap
> That man cry out who cannot sleep:
> "If God is God He is not good,
> If God is good He is not God."[2]

The term "theodicy" was coined by the German mathematician and philosopher Gottfried Wilhelm von Leibniz in his 1710 book, *Theodicy: Essays on the Goodness of God, the Freedom of Man and the Origin of Evil.* Like the mathematician that he was, Leibniz cast his defenses of both God's goodness and His justice as a series of formal syllogisms, concluding that God is both benevolent and all-powerful, and that the world is therefore the best it could possibly be. God allows people to suffer as a necessary consequence of the freedom that must exist in the best of all possible worlds. The common name for Leibniz's philosophical position is "optimism," which means the belief that God has optimized the world's potential; it is not, as the more popular usage of the term suggests, the belief that we should always look on the bright side of things.

Logically, the philosophy of optimism addresses the problem of evil straightforwardly by denying that evil exists in the world. In formal logic, the problem is expressed as a deductive syllogism that goes something like this:

- **Major Premise:** If there is a God who is omnibenevolent and omnipotent, then evil should not exist.
- **Minor Premise:** Evil exists.
- **Conclusion:** There is not an omnipotent, omnibenevolent God.

Leibniz solves the problem by disputing the minor premise. The human perspective, he suggests, cannot adequately judge good and evil on the universal scale. We call things "evil" from our tragically limited point of view. But from God's perspective, what we perceive as evil is actually, not merely good, but perfect. Leibniz's most famous popularizer, Alexander

---

2. Archibald MacLeish, *J.B.*, 11.

Pope, made this the basis of his eighteenth-century poetic theodicy, "An Essay on Man,"a famous passage of which reads:

> All Nature is but Art, unknown to thee;
> All Chance, Direction, which thou canst not see;
> All Discord, Harmony, not understood;
> All partial Evil, universal Good:
> And, spite of Pride, in erring Reason's spite,
> One truth is clear, "Whatever IS, is RIGHT."[3]

Contemporaries of Leibniz and Pope did not always share these views. The great French writer Voltaire savagely parodied Leibniz as Dr. Pangloss ("all-tongue") in his 1759 satiric novella, *Candide*. The novella opens with Dr. Pangloss tutoring the young hero, Candide, in the philosophy of optimism. His refrain, which becomes the ironic focal point of the novel, is drawn straight from Leibniz: "all is for the best in this best of all possible worlds." Throughout the novel, Candide experiences the worst that the world has to offer: wars, earthquakes, the Inquisition, deceit and destruction. The more Candide tries to fit everything that happens to him into the optimistic narrative, the less seriously readers can take the effort. At the very end of the narrative, Candide rejects Pangloss' philosophy and decides to settle down in one place and tend his small garden—enjoying the life that is instead of speculating on the life that should be.

Candide is a Job story. Voltaire himself acknowledged this in a letter to Frederick the Great of Prussia in which he affirmed that his famous satire was "Job brought up to date."[4] It contains most of the essential elements of Job: deprivation, physical torment, extreme misfortune, and philosophical quarrels about the nature of the universe. But Voltaire does not have God speak from a whirlwind to bring the narrative to a conclusion. Instead, he gives us a whirling dervish—a holy man of Istanbul with whom Candide converses in the final chapter. When Candide asks the dervish why God allows evil in the world, he responds with a rhetorical question, "When His Highness sends a ship to Egypt, do you suppose he worries about whether the ship's mice are comfortable or not?"[5] On the strength of this view of God, we can call *Candide* a theodicy, albeit not a particularly joyous one.

Voltaire solves the problem of evil by disputing the major premise. A confirmed Deist, Voltaire believed in a "Clockmaker God"—one who

---

3. Alexander Pope, *Poetry and Prose of Alexander Pope*, 130.
4. Mark Larrimore, *The Book of Job: A Biography*, 162.
5. See Voltaire, *Candide*.

established the physical laws of the universe and then ceased to play an active role in its affairs. Candide encounters no divine influence in his journeys because there is no divine influence to encounter. Voltaire's God may or may not be omnipotent, but He is certainly not benevolent in any sense of the word that humans can understand. Our suffering does not move Him, and our sense of justice does not impress Him. Things happen because they happen, and God takes no interest in human affairs.

Many nineteenth- and twentieth-century interpretations of Job borrow freely from the positions of both Leibniz and Voltaire to address the problem of evil. The main thrust of these interpretations is that God simply cannot be held to human standards of morality. This could mean (following Leibniz) that we cannot see how perfect God's actions are unless we see how all of the pieces fit together—with the implication that, if we could see the whole picture, we would recognize the moral perfection of all things. Just as often, however, it means that God operates according to standards of morality that human beings cannot possibly comprehend—ever. Friedrich Nietzsche provided the vocabulary for this view, though certainly not the theology, with the term "beyond good and evil." The great British classicist Gilbert Murray employs this vocabulary directly in his 1940 analysis of Job:

> God does not show, or even say, that He is righteous by human standards of righteousness; what he does assert is that He is, in Nietzsche's phrase. . . Beyond Good and Evil, and that the puny standards by which man judges right and wrong simply do not apply to the power that rules the universe. If God's rule conflicts with human morality, that is because human morality is such a limited thing, not valid beyond certain regions of time and space. It is impertinence in man to expect God to be "righteous."[6]

These basic themes appear throughout the interpretations of Job in the nineteenth and the first half of the twentieth century, as Job shows how small the human perspective is, how great God is, and how foolish it is for us to think that we can use our human standards of morality to judge God. God sees everything, everywhere, and everywhen. We see only a small fragment of space and time; our vision is so colored by our own perspective that we cannot formulate a definition of "good" and "evil" comprehensive enough to force God into our syllogisms.

Such sentiments can certainly be inferred from God's final speech. I inferred many of them myself in Chapter Six. But there are some prob-

---

6. Nahum N. Glatzer, ed., *The Dimensions of Job*, 196.

lems with asserting, as the ultimate meaning of the poem, that God's ways are so big and so mysterious that we can never approach him as anything other than mice on the decks of his boats—beginning with the fact that it is a really depressing message. This doesn't mean it is not what the author intended. But if all I can derive from Job is a greater understanding of my own worthless nothingness, then the game just isn't worth the candle. Voltaire can tell me the same thing in a fraction of the time, and I won't even have to read poetry.

A more significant problem with this line of interpretation is that it makes about half of the poem unnecessary. Job acknowledges God's great power and unfathomable understanding at the outset, and his Comforters play the "how dare you presume to question God's ways" card in almost every speech. The vastness of God's perspective is the main point of the Hymn to Wisdom in chapter 28, and the impossibility of ever understanding God's motives is a main theme of Elihu's speeches in chapters 32 through 35. The poet does not have to bring God on stage to say that He is great and Job is nothing. In fact, God's appearance in the poem works directly against such a message. The very fact that God talks to Job undermines the argument that God is far too busy and important to go around talking to inconsequential nobodies like Job.

Finally, and most importantly, "God's ways are not your ways" is just too much of an easy cliché about human suffering to be the main point of a poem designed to dismantle easy clichés about human suffering. This is why Job's Comforters say it so frequently. It is a smart-sounding generalization that cannot easily be refuted, and it effectively tells sufferers that they should quit complaining. This is why Job has functioned for centuries as a way to silence complaints. When somebody complains too loudly about their lot in life, we can always assure them that they are not as bad off as Job—with the clear implication that they should quit their bellyaching and just decide to be happy. God himself says as much to Joseph Smith in Liberty Jail when He says, "Thou art not yet as Job; thy friends do not contend against thee, neither charge thee with transgression, as they did Job" (D&C 121:10).

This might be a good way to respond to a moderately difficult situation, such as having to spend a few months in jail, but it falls flat in the face of profound suffering—which is why this way of reading Job as a theodicy did not survive the twentieth century intact. During the Holocaust and the other cataclysmic events of the mid-twentieth century, huge swaths of humanity—including nearly every member of the European Jewish community—suffered in ways that equaled and exceeded the suffering of Job.

In the world that the Holocaust helped to create, "God is great and we are nothing" just won't work as an answer to the question, "Why do the innocent suffer?" And "you are not as bad off as Job" has become a tragic lie.

God on Trial

In his classic Holocaust memoir *Night*, Elie Wiesel recalls that, after three weeks in Auschwitz, he could no longer pray. "I concurred with Job," Wiesel writes, "I was not denying [God's] existence, but I doubted His absolute justice."[7] This is the reader's first glimpse of Wiesel's faith crisis, which becomes a major theme of the book and of Wiesel's later work. Shortly after coming to this conclusion, Wiesel writes, he witnessed the celebration of Rosh Hashanah—the Jewish New Year—in the Buna work camp associated with Auschwitz. The fifteen-year-old Wiesel could not participate in the tradition of blessing the Lord's name because he had already reached the conclusion that God did not deserve his blessings:

> Why, but why would I bless Him? Every fiber in me rebelled. Because He caused thousands of children to burn in His mass graves? Because He kept six crematoria working day and night, including Sabbath and the Holy Days? Because in His great might, He had created Auschwitz, Birkenau, Buna, and so many other factories of death? How could I say to Him: Blessed be Thou, Almighty, Master of the Universe, who chose us among all nations to be tortured day and night, to watch as our fathers, our mothers, our brothers end up in the furnaces? Praised be Thy Holy Name, for having chosen us to be slaughtered on Thine altar? . . . In days gone by, Rosh Hashanah had dominated my life. I knew that my sins grieved the Almighty and so I pleaded for forgiveness. In those days, I fully believed that the salvation of the world depended on every one of my deeds, on every one of my prayers. . . . But now, I no longer pleaded for anything. I was no longer able to lament. On the contrary, I felt very strong. I was the accuser, God the accused.[8]

The theme of God as the accused becomes a major theme in Wiesel's subsequent writing, and the Book of Job becomes a major part of his argument. In his 1976 book *Messengers of God*, Wiesel acknowledges that, after the war, he was "preoccupied with Job. . . . In those days he could be seen on every road of Europe." But he refuses to accept the canonical ending in

---

7. Elie Wiesel, *Night*, 45. This translation by Wiesel's wife, Marion, supersedes Stella Rodway's 1960 translation of the 1958 French text *La Nuit*, published by Les Éditions de Minuit in Paris.

8. Wiesel, *Night*, 67–68.

which Job repents and acknowledges God's goodness. This, Wiesel argues, "was an insult to man." The ending of Job must be rewritten to account for the Holocaust. "He should have said to God, very well, I forgive You, I forgive You to the extent of my sorrow, my anguish. But what about my dead children. . . .What right do I have to speak on their behalf?"[9]

Wiesel's Job goes on to demand the justice that Job demands in both the Wisdom dialogue and in his final speech. "By accepting your inequities," he asks God, "do I not become Your accomplice? Now it is my turn to choose between You and my children, and I refuse to repudiate them. I demand that justice be done to them, if not to me, and that the trial continue." In Wiesel's imagined ending—which simply extends Job's defiance throughout the poem into the epilogue—Job becomes the hero who challenges God in the name of humanity. "Thanks to him, we know that it is given to man to transform divine injustice into human justice and compassion."[10]

One compelling experience that Wiesel had in Auschwitz—and which does not appear in *Night*—became the basis of his best-known stage play. "Inside the kingdom of night," he wrote much later, "I witnessed a strange trial. Three rabbis—all erudite and pious men—decided one winter evening to indict God for allowing his children to be massacred. I remember: I was there, and I felt like crying. But there nobody cried."[11] Though not set in Auschwitz or in the twentieth century, Wiesel's play, *The Trial of God*, is based on the premise of indicting God for crimes against humanity.

Wiesel sets his trial in the Ukrainian village of Shamgorod in 1649, two years after nearly all of the Jews in the village had been murdered in a pogrom.[12] The only two survivors—the innkeeper Bearish and his daughter Hannah—run a small inn for travelers. Hannah has been so scarred by the pogrom that she rarely leaves her room. Bearish, who lost his wife and all of his sons in the violence, has become an inveterate hater of God. As Wiesel states in a later interview, "Bearish is very close to Job. He has lost nearly everything."[13] Of himself, Bearish says, "I resigned from

---

9. Elie Wiesel, *Messengers of God*, 233–34.

10. Ibid., 234–35.

11. Elie Wiesel, *The Trial of God*, unpaginated stage direction before the play begins.

12. As Wiesel would later explain in an interview, he invented the village of "Shamgorod" from the Hebrew word for "to scrape," which is used only once in the Bible to describe Job scraping his sores with a potshard. The name of the town literally translates into "there he scraped," making it, allegorically, the site of Job's dialogue with his friends. See Tod Linafelt, ed., *Strange Fire: Reading the Bible after the Holocaust*, 31.

13. Ibid., 30.

membership in God—I resigned from God. Let Him look for another innkeeper, let Him find another people, let Him push around another Jew. I'm through with Him."[14]

As the play begins, three Jewish men come into Bearish's Inn seeking food and rest. The men are *Purimschpielers*, or actors who travel through the countryside performing farcical plays to celebrate Purim. In typical fashion, they seek to exchange a *Purimschpiel* for their meal and lodging, but Bearish won't have it. He has no use for the traditional Purim stories of Esther and Mordecai, or for any of the other Bible stories that the players know. There is only one drama that Bearish will accept as payment for his services: "Let's stage a trial" he tells them, "Against the Master of the universe! Against the Supreme Judge! That is the spectacle you shall stage tonight."[15]

The hungry and tired *Purimschpielers* agree. They will be the jury, and Bearish will be the prosecutor, but nobody volunteers to defend God until a mysterious stranger named Sam steps forward to offer his services. Gradually, Sam is revealed to be Satan—not quite the figure of pure evil that Christians believe in, but the Satan of Job, "God's emissary" whose job is to "visit His creation and bring stories back to Him."[16] Thus, in Wiesel's reconstruction of Job, everybody trades places: God becomes the accused, the Accuser becomes the defender, the Job figure becomes the accuser, and the Comforters become the judges. The world of Job is turned inside out and upside down—precisely as it should be in the carnivalesque atmosphere of a *Purimschpiel*.

In practice, Sam/Satan resembles nothing so much as an academic theologian invoking the standard theodicy arguments. "Men and women and other children were massacred by other men," he submits, "why implicate their father in heaven?" And he rejects both the evil and the finality of death, as the dead "form an immense community reposing in God and loving Him the way you have never loved and never will!" When Bearish asks how a father could stand by while his children were being massacred, Sam responds with the most common theodicy argument of all: "God is God, and His will is independent from ours—as is His reasoning."[17] "Satan knew the answer," Wiesel later explained, "he has all the answers. Actually, Satan speaks like a fanatic. . . . The fanatic thinks he is justifying God."[18]

---

14. Wiesel, *The Trial of God*, 15.
15. Ibid., 55.
16. Ibid., 158.
17. Ibid., 131–32.
18. Linafelt, *Strange Fire*, 31.

The question of God's guilt is never determined in the play. Before the jury can return a verdict, the people of Shamgorod burst in on the proceedings to finish what they started two years earlier. The lights go down as Satan reveals himself as the author of a new pogrom. Tellingly, this new outburst of violence takes the place of God's speech from the whirlwind at the end of Job. Here, we have neither the revelation of the poem or the restoration of the frame—but just God's silence, punctuated by another round of senseless butchery. God is absent from the entire proceeding. Instead of the voice of God, we get Behemoth and Leviathan run amok. Violence and murder become the only answer to Bearish's questions—and the only responses to the author's accusations against God.

God for Grown-Ups

In the vernacular of formal logic, Elie Wiesel solves the theodicy problem the same way that Voltaire does: by rejecting the part of the major premise that requires an omnibenevolent deity. Wiesel's God is not perfectly benevolent; He is not even very nice. And after the Holocaust, He can no longer ask us to trust Him. As Wiesel writes in *Day*, the third book in the *Night Trilogy*, "Man prefers to blame himself for all possible sins and crimes rather than come to the conclusion that God is capable of the most flagrant injustice."[19] Like Job, Wiesel never denies God—but he certainly doesn't like Him much.

An opinion similar to Wiesel's—but with subtle, yet important differences—can be found in one of the most remarkable works of Holocaust literature ever produced. Since its initial publication in 1946, the short story "Yosl Rakover Talks to God" has had nearly as strange and wonderful of a journey as the Book of Job, on which it is based. The story's author, Zvi Kolitz, was a refugee from the once-prosperous Lithuanian Jewish community that was utterly destroyed by the one-two punch of Stalin and Hitler. Kolitz lived briefly in Argentina before immigrating to Israel, where he became a successful film director, and eventually ending up in New York, where he died in 2002 at the age of eighty-nine. For most of his life, Kolitz watched helplessly as the 5,000-word story he wrote in his youth took on a life of its own without him.

"Yosl Rakover Talks to God" was clearly marked as fiction when it first appeared in an obscure Buenos Aires newspaper. But it is exactly the

---

19. Elie Wiesel, *Day*, 34.

kind of story that could easily be mistaken for a historical document if separated from its original context. It presents itself as the final testimony of a Jew who took part in the Warsaw Ghetto uprising in 1943. It is also a Job story. Like Job, Yosl has seen all of his children die and all of his possessions destroyed. "Like Job," he says, "I can say of myself—naked shall I return unto the earth." And like Job, he never loses his faith in God. In fact, he steadfastly refuses to allow divine indifference to affect his own faith, and he determines to love God whether or not He deserves it. Consider the following two passages:

> I believe in the God of Israel, even when He has done everything to make me cease to believe in Him. I believe in His laws even when I cannot justify His deeds. My relationship to Him is no longer that of a servant to his master, but of a student to his rabbi. I bow my head before His greatness, but I will not kiss the rod with which He chastises me.[20]

And, addressing God directly, he says,

> You . . . are doing everything to make me cease believing in You. But if You think that You will succeed with these trials in deflecting me from the true path, then I cry to You, my God and the God of my parents, that none of it will help You. You may insult me, You may chastise me, You may take from me the dearest and the best that I have in the world, You may torture me to death—I will always believe in You. I will love You always and forever—even despite You.[21]

Through an amazing series of events, "Yosl Rakover Talks to God" found its way to Israel where it was published in 1954 as a factual recollection called "A Testament from the Warsaw Ghetto." From there, it was translated into German, French, and English and published to great acclaim throughout Europe and America. On several occasions, Kolitz wrote letters to newspapers or publishers explaining that he was the author of the text and that it was a work of fiction, but the letters were ignored. People wanted the story to be true, and so it became true. It was not until the literary detective work of Paul Badde in the mid 1990s that Kolitz received credit for his story.

Perhaps the most important moment in the life of the Yosl Rakover myth occurred in 1963, when the great philosopher Emmanuel Levinas published a brief essay on the story in a French magazine. Levinas, also a Lithuanian Jew, immigrated to France in 1931 and spent much of World War II as a Jewish POW in a German prison camp. Unlike most of his

---

20. Zvi Kolitz, *Yosl Rakover Talks to God*, 17–18.
21. Ibid., 24.

contemporaries, Levinas immediately recognized the story as a fiction (albeit an anonymous one), which, he argued, made it "both beautiful and true, true as only fiction can be."[22] For Levinas, "Yosl Rakover Talks to God" created a portrait of "a grown man's God" who "shows himself in the very emptiness of a childish heaven."[23] Children relate to God the way they relate to their parents: they see them as both omni-competent and omni-benevolent—and they cry a good deal when they don't get what they want. Levinas describes the God that we worship this way as a "kindergarten deity who distributed prizes, applied penalties, or forgave faults and in His goodness treated men as eternal children."[24]

Levinas argued that God needs grown-ups. He understands that a God worshipped only by children can never experience the absolute love of His creations—as a child's love is always conditional. "His divine grandeur," Levinas writes, "is shown in his creation of a man capable of approaching God as a creditor and not always as a debtor. The creditor has faith in abundance, but also does not resign himself to the evasions of the debtor."[25] God's majesty, then, requires people who worship him as spiritual adults rather than perpetual children—people who ask for reasons, who demand justice, and who refuse to accept "because God said so" as a final answer.

God, in other words, wants his children to worship him as Job does, not as the Comforters do. This may be the only way to explain the epilogue as a logical continuation of the poem.[26] Immediately after the poem concludes, Yahweh turns to Eliphaz and says, "I am incensed at you and your two friends, for you have not spoken the truth about Me as did My servant Job" (42:7). This is somewhat ironic, given that the Comforters are one hundred percent on God's side the whole time. They defend His honor tirelessly, and they criticize Job the most when he disputes God's justice or goodness. If we throw Elihu into the mix, the Comforters start to look more like God's cheerleaders than Job's friends. And yet God rebukes them and sustains Job.

---

22. Ibid., 80.

23. Ibid., 84.

24. Ibid., 81.

25. Ibid., 85–86.

26. As I suggest in Chapter 3, of course, it is very possible that the Epilogue is not meant to be a logical continuation of the poem. It belongs to the world of the frame and may only be commenting on the actions of the Comforters in the first two chapters. This is a difficult argument to sustain, however, in light of the fact that the Comforters do not actually say anything in the first two chapters.

The philosopher Immanuel Kant suggests a reason for God's rebuke. The Comforters, Kant suggests, "speak as if they were being secretly listened to by the mighty one . . . as if gaining his favor through their judgment were closer to their heart than the truth."[27] Job, on the other hand, does little more than complain about God for the whole poem—accusing Him, among other things, of injustice, incompetence, and impure motives. But in the end, God tells the Comforters only, "you have not spoken the truth about Me as did My servant Job." Job's God seems to make it clear that He would rather we challenge Him vigorously than affirm Him uncritically.

I have found this sentiment in nearly all of the great teachers and inspiring leaders I have ever known. Weak leaders crave praise from their followers, and insecure teachers want their students to sit down and shut up. But the truly great ones—leaders and teachers who are confident in their abilities and secure in their position—want to be challenged. They can accept correction when it is genuinely called for, and even when it is not, they know that people need to test their ideas in order to progress. If God were not of this mind Himself, He would hardly have ended his time on stage praising the man who criticized Him—or rebuking the three men who spent the whole poem sucking up.

This is the God that Wiesel and Levinas present to us in their interpretations of Job. They believe that human beings—and especially human beings who have suffered greatly—have both a right and a responsibility to present to God the demands of humanity. For Levinas, though, this is not an existential tragedy, but an invitation to spiritual adulthood. As children, we see our parents as infallible. As adults, we recognize that they are not, and we learn that we can still love and honor them while challenging them to do better. "God must reveal His face," Levinas demands, "justice and power must be reconnected, there must be just institutions on this earth. Only he who has recognized the veiled face of God can demand that it be unveiled."[28] Recognizing God when He is in disguise and demanding that He unveil his face are things that only grown-ups can do.

The Limited God

Wiesel, Kolitz, and Levinas all address the problem of evil by questioning God's goodness. They grant Him absolute power but insist that He has not used it ethically to prevent great tragedies, such as the Holocaust.

27. Immanuel Kant, "On the Miscarriage of All Philosophical Trials in Theodicy," 32.
28. Kolitz, *Yosl Rakover Talks to God*, 86.

A second way to address the problem is to dispute God's omnipotence. According to the terms of the syllogism, one can reconcile an omnibenevolent God with the evil in the world by demonstrating ways in which God's power is limited. This argument can take several forms—some of them quite familiar to Latter-day Saints, such as the idea that God is bound by eternal laws that He cannot or will not violate. If God is subject to any such constraints, then the major premise ("there is a God who is omnibenevolent and omnipotent") cannot be true.

Some of the most notable post-Holocaust interpreters of Job, both Jewish and Christian, also solve the theodicy problem by invoking some version of the assertion that God does not have the power to prevent evil all of the time. This, in fact, is the conclusion of the book with which this chapter began, Rabbi Harold Kushner's *When Bad Things Happen to Good People*:

> Let me suggest that the author of the Book of Job takes the position which neither Job nor his friends take. He believes in God's goodness and in Job's goodness, and is prepared to give up his belief in proposition (A): that God is all-powerful. Bad things do happen to good people in this world, but it is not God who wills it. God would like people to get what they deserve in life, but He cannot always arrange it. Forced to choose between a good God who is not totally powerful, or a powerful God who is not totally good, the author of the Book of Job chooses to believe in God's goodness.[29]

More than thirty years after writing *When Bad Things Happen to Good People*, Kushner expanded this argument significantly for his book-length treatment of Job, *The Book of Job: When Bad Things Happened to a Good Person* (2012). For Kushner, this argument is supported by a careful reading of God's second speech to Job, which details God's dealings with Behemoth and Leviathan. These two beasts, Kushner argues, "represent forces of the created world with which even God Himself is challenged to contend. They are necessary dimensions of God's world . . . But even God has to exert himself to keep them from getting out of hand."[30]

Kushner reads both mythological beasts allegorically: Behemoth represents human ambition—our urge to conquer and colonize and acquire whatever we desire. Leviathan represents chaos and randomness. The world could not exist without these forces, but they also have the power to unleash great destruction. In Kushner's interpretation, Job's God is saddened by the evil that exists in the world, but He realizes—and expects Job to realize—that the forces that create this evil are neces-

---

29. Harold Kushner, *When Bad Things Happen to Good People*, 42–43.

30. Harold Kushner, *The Book of Job: When Bad Things Happened to a Good Person*, 146.

sary parts of creation that He must constantly keep in check. He can contain, but not eliminate, the suffering that these forces cause.

We find a much different version of the limited God in Archibald MacLeish's *J.B.*, perhaps the most well-known twentieth-century adaptation of Job. *J.B.* was first performed in New Haven in 1958 before moving to Broadway in 1959 for a production that won both the Tony Award and the Pulitzer Prize. The title character is a wealthy and devout financer with a beautiful wife and five devoted children. The bulk of the play recreates the frame narrative of Job, as J.B. loses his fortune and watches helplessly as each of his children die in horrible ways. After each child dies, J.B. affirms his faith in the goodness of God.

The dialogue between God and Satan occupies much more space in *J.B.* than it does in Job. The two are not actually the eternal beings we see in Job; they are former actors now working as circus vendors, and they take it upon themselves to stage Job in a deserted circus tent. Mr. Zuss, who sells balloons, takes on the role of God, while Mr. Nickles, a popcorn vendor, is cast as Satan. They set out to stage Job as they know it from the Bible. This conception of God sets the stage (quite literally) for MacLeish's reinterpretation of Job. Like Job, God is locked in a role that He cannot change and does not fully understand. And, like Job, His assigned role is constantly at war with His human emotions.

The relationship between Mr. Zuss (God) and Mr. Nickles (Satan) neatly reverses the relationship in the Job frame. Nickles initially believes that he will play Job, but Zuss tells him to choose another role, since "there's always someone playing Job."[31] He settles for the role of Satan, but he continues to identify with Job. Thus, the character playing Satan becomes the play's humanist. He is much more affected than Zuss at the deaths of J.B.'s children, and he actively tries to get J.B. to renounce his faith in God—not because he wants to win the bet, but because he thinks God does not deserve J.B.'s loyalty. As J.B. continues to praise God after each of his trials, Nickles (Satan) becomes furious with God for allowing the man to suffer:

> I think it stinks!
> One daughter raped and murdered by an idiot,
> Another crushed by stones, a son
> Destroyed by some fool officer's stupidity,
> Two children smeared across a road
> At midnight by a drunken child -

---

31. MacLeish, *J.B.*, 12.

And all with God's consent! - foreknowledge! -
And he blesses God! It isn't decent!
It isn't moral even! It's disgusting!
His weeping wife in her despair
And he beside her on his trembling ham-bones
Praising God! . . . It's nauseating![32]

But Satan loses the bet, as he must. J.B. remains faithful to God. But when he does, we see a remarkable transformation in Zuss (God), who cannot believe that J.B. loved Him enough to remain faithful through all of his trials. He begins weeping and expressing gratitude in the knowledge that Job repented and praised God, not out of any expectation of reward or punishment, but simply out of love. "In spite of everything he'd suffered! / In spite of all he'd lost and loved / *He* understood and he forgave it."[33] In MacLeish's finale, J.B. forgives God, and God, in gratitude, offers to restore all that he once had. But J.B. refuses and sets out with his wife to make a new life for himself. And it is God, not Job, who is healed in the end.

During the time that he was writing *J.B.*, but before it was ever performed, Archibald MacLeish delivered a sermon on Job to a church in Farmington, Connecticut. The sermon, entitled "God Has Need of Man," lays out much of the theology that finds its way into the final scenes of *J.B.* God, MacLeish suggests, needs the love of His creations. "Without man's love, God does not exist as God, only as creator, and love is the one thing no one, not even God Himself, can command. It is a free gift, or it is nothing." The need for human love is not merely about feeding God's ego; the stakes are unimaginably high: "Satan, who is the denial of life . . . cannot be overcome by God who is his opposite, who is the kingdom of life, except by man's persistence in the love of God."[34]

If this is true, then Satan's challenge to God at the beginning of Job was a challenge that He had to answer forcefully. If human beings love God only conditionally, then He is not God. We must remember that MacLeish is a literary critic interpreting a poem and not a historian trying to explain why the real God consented to the suffering of the real Job. But even if he were the latter, I suspect, his answer would not change much: God permits good people to suffer because, if He followed the so-called Law of the Harvest and rewarded everybody according to their faithful-

---

32. Ibid., *J.B.*, 93.
33. Ibid., *J.B.*, 139.
34. Archibald MacLeish, "God Has Need of Man," 285.

ness, then he would never experience the unconditional, freely given love that allows Him to be God. And Satan would then win the universe.

God Can Take It

Suffering on the scale of the Holocaust deepens the problem of evil by expanding our understanding of evil's reach. And it calls forth new interpretations of the ancient poem most associated with suffering. For us to see Job as any kind of theodicy in the post-Holocaust world, we must find new ways to inhabit the text. We cannot read into it assurances that things will work out for us in the end if we just trust God, for things do not always work out. Interpretations of Job that do no more than confirm the absolute wonderfulness of God simply do not speak to the pain and suffering of real people.

In *Negative Dialectics*, the German-Jewish exile Theodor Adorno wrote, "the need to let suffering speak is a condition of all truth."[35] Those of us who choose to believe in a benevolent and powerful God, despite the suffering that we see all around us, have a sacred responsibility to meet Adorno's condition faithfully. We cannot use God, or our belief in God, to dismiss other people's pain. Sometimes, this means listening to things that make us uncomfortable or challenge our beliefs. It means allowing people to speak ill of things that we think well of—including (and perhaps especially) ourselves. And it means listening compassionately to those who criticize, contradict, or seek justice from God or from the human institutions that claim to represent Him. God can take care of Himself; our responsibility is to take care of each other.

To meet our obligations to our fellow human beings, we need not believe that God is lacking in either power or goodness. We just need to understand that He does not require our assistance in dealing with challenges to His authority. We do not have to protect God from criticisms, complaints, and petitions. He is not some little first-time godling out on a test drive. He can take criticism. He can handle complaints. And He has no need to fear when human beings ask Him to do things differently. Too many people—often from positions of ecclesiastical authority—spend their time trying to make sure that God's feelings do not get hurt. This is how we become the Comforters when we should be listening—really listening with our hearts—to the suffering Job.

---

35. Theodor W. Adorno, *Negative Dialectics*, 17–18.

Chapter Ten

Job and the Wisdom Tradition

How different the man who devotes himself
to the study of the law of the Most High!
He explores the wisdom of the men of old
and occupies himself with the prophecies;
He treasures the discourses of famous men,
and goes to the heart of involved sayings;
He studies obscure parables,
and is busied with the hidden meanings of the sages.
He is in attendance on the great,
and has entrance to the ruler.
He travels among the peoples of foreign lands
to learn what is good and evil among men.
    —Sirach 39:15 (NAB)

Wisdom in Israelite Religion

We can say very little with certainty about the religion of the Ancient Hebrews, including whether or not they had a religion at all. Most of the people of the Ancient Near East worshipped their national god or gods, to whom they had certain responsibilities including offering sacrifices, holding festivals, observing ritual prohibitions, and reciting prayers. Such activities were religious, but they were not necessarily a "religion" that could be separated from any other part of a person's life. It was simply what one did.

The Ancient Hebrews were no exception. The national deity of both the Northern Kingdom (Israel) and the Southern Kingdom (Judah) was known by the four consonants YHWH. Early English translations of the Bible, over influenced by Latin and lacking a firm grasp of classical Hebrew, rendered the name as "Jehovah." Scholars now believe that the name was pronounced more like "Yahweh" and that worshippers of Yahweh competed for public and political favor with worshippers of other Near-Eastern deities of Canaanite origin. Both internal and external evidence suggests that, shortly before the destruction of Jerusalem by the Babylonian Empire, Yahweh-worship expanded dramatically during the long reign of King Josiah (641–609 B.C.), a pro-Yahweh reformer who outlawed all other forms of worship (see 2 Kings 22–23; 2 Chron. 34–35).

Because the Josianic reformation occurred only a few years before the destruction of Jerusalem, the Jewish exiles in Babylon were stronger in their devotion to Yahweh than their ancestors had been at any time in history. Remarkably, they became even more devoted to their national god when they no longer had a nation. Judaism as a religion first began to take shape among the exile community in Babylon. When the Persians conquered Babylon in 539 B.C., the Jews were allowed to return to Jerusalem, but most of them did not; they preferred to remain in Cyrus the Great's relatively tolerant Achaemenid Empire, where they assembled and edited their sacred texts into the book that Christians now call the Old Testament.

Modern scholarship suggests that three very distinct schools of Ancient Hebrew thought participated in the construction of the Tanakh: the Deuteronomistic school, the Priestly school, and the Wisdom school.[1] We should not consider these separate denominations of Judaism; rather, they were different, but often overlapping, strands of Ancient Hebrew thought that went into the creation of Judaism. And each school looked for guidance to a different ideal figure in Hebrew society. For the Deuteronomists, this was the Prophet; for the Priestly school, the Priest; and for the Wisdom school, the Sage.

The Deuteronomistic school—so called because it crafted the Book of Deuteronomy, or the "Second Law"—focused on the special relationship between Yahweh and the people of Israel. They saw that relationship as a sacred covenant that would lead to their prosperity if they honored it and their destruction if they did not. During the Babylonian exile, Deuteronomistic editors and redactors forged a comprehensive history of Israel—comprising most of the historical information between Joshua and 2 Kings—that highlighted the covenant between God and their ancestors. And they framed that history as constant struggle between God's prophets and the wayward people of Israel. We have already seen (in Chapter Seven) how the author of the Book of Job rejected much of the Deuteronomistic orthodoxy of his day.

---

1. For an overview of the three religious schools and their place in Ancient Hebrew religion, see Stephen A. Geller's essay "The Religion of the Bible," 2021–40.

The second group, the Priestly school, emphasized sacrifice and ritual purity. They were primarily concerned with correct forms of worship, something rarely mentioned by the Deuteronomists. Priestly writers and editors created the Book of Leviticus in order to preserve their accumulated knowledge about proper sacrificial techniques, and they also contributed portions to all of the other books in the Pentateuch—including the first chapter of Genesis and the last chapter of Deuteronomy, leading many scholars to conclude that Priestly redactors had the final editorial say over the construction of the *Torah*.[2]

The final school of Ancient Hebrew thought—and by far the most difficult one to define—was the Wisdom school, or the school of the sages. Prophets and priests wrote themselves into the story. We see the prophets interacting with the people throughout the Old Testament, and we know precisely what the priests did because, in the Book of Leviticus, they left behind their instruction manual. Though they may well have been equally important to the ancient Hebrew society, sages left far fewer fingerprints on the Tanakh.

But we can reconstruct their role from a number of different textual and contextual sources. We know, for example, that Wisdom teachers existed throughout the Ancient Near East. They advised political rulers and tutored the children of the wealthy and powerful. They played a prominent enough role in other Semitic societies that it would have been anomalous if they had not been part of Hebrew culture too—probably in important positions in the court.[3] We see occasional negative references in the prophetic books to "wise men" who have rejected the Lord (Isa. 5:21; Jer. 8:8–9). And we have a small, but very influential corpus of wisdom literature in the Old Testament whose theology appears fundamentally at odds with both the Deuteronomistic and the Priestly narratives favored in the same time period.

As Old Testament scholar James L. Crenshaw suggests, "the existence of a body of literature that reflects specific interests at variance with Yahwistic texts in general seems to argue strongly for a professional class of sages in Israel." Books like Job and Ecclesiastes often appear to work against the Deuteronomistic and priestly traditions simultaneously, and even the Book of Proverbs has nothing to say about ritual purity or about

---

2. See David Bokovoy's *Authoring the Old Testament: Genesis–Deuteronomy* for an excellent description of both the Priestly (42–51) and the Deuteronomistic (62–70) sources of the first five books of the Hebrew Bible.

3. See John G. Gammie and Leo G. Purdue, eds., *The Sage in Israel and the Ancient Near East.*

the great prophetic heroes of the Yahwistic tradition. Instead, Crenshaw argues, "the reader encounters in these three books a *different world of thought*, one that stands apart so impressively that some scholars have described that literary corpus as an alien body within the Bible."[4]

Unlike those in the other schools, the Wisdom writers do not appear to have shared a common philosophical or theological outlook. The principal Wisdom books differ as much from each other as they do from the other books in the Hebrew Bible. Occasionally they even work against each other directly, as Proverbs and Ecclesiastes do. But they share enough common elements to allow us to talk about them as part of a coherent school of thought. These elements include the following:

> **Wisdom literature is pragmatic:** The main function of Wisdom literature is to help people live better lives. This means learning how to deal with big issues, like the fear of death or the reality of suffering. But it also means learning how to negotiate relationships with other people, please employers, manage employees, stay healthy, raise good children, and live a meaningful life. The Wisdom literature of the Bible has something to say about all of the issues and many more. Understanding this brings us close to Crenshaw's definition of "Wisdom" as "the reasoned search for specific ways to ensure personal well-being in everyday life, to make sense of extreme adversity and vexing anomalies, and to transmit this hard-earned knowledge so that successive generations will embody it."[5]

> **Wisdom literature is experiential:** The German theologian Gerhard von Rad begins his groundbreaking book, *Wisdom in Israel*, with the observation that "Every nation with a culture has devoted itself to the care and the literary cultivation of . . . experiential knowledge and has carefully gathered its statements in the form of sentence-type proverbs. This, then, is one of the most elementary functions of the human mind."[6] For the Ancient Hebrews, Wisdom literature served this essential purpose. It collected the culture's tried and true experiential knowledge about a wide range of topics and put them into memorable sound bites that could be easily learned and long remembered.

> **Wisdom literature is literary:** In addition to the three principal Wisdom books of the *Kethuvim*—Job, Proverbs, and Ecclesiastes—scholars have identified wisdom components in a handful of the Psalms, in the stories

4. James L. Crenshaw, *Old Testament Wisdom: An Introduction*, 21.

5. Ibid., 3.

6. Gerhard Von Rad, *Wisdom in Israel*, 4.

of Joseph and Jonah, and in the Books of Ruth, Esther, Lamentations, and the Song of Solomon. The deuterocanonical books of Wisdom and Sirach are also considered Wisdom books. Not coincidentally, these are the parts of the Old Testament that many people consider works of literature—either short stories such as Ruth and Esther, poems such as Psalms and Job, or collections of literary aphorisms such as Proverbs and Ecclesiastes. More than any other kind of scripture, Wisdom literature lends itself to literary expression, as the ability to understand literary forms (i.e., to be "busied with the hidden meaning of the sages") is one of the hallmarks of true wisdom.

Wisdom literature is international: In an essay on Hebrew religion included in the Jewish Study Bible, Stephen A. Geller explains that the Wisdom tradition was not unique to Ancient Israel. Wisdom schools and Wisdom teachers flourished throughout Egypt and Mesopotamia in the ancient world, and we can find clear borrowings from these sources in the biblical texts. This should not surprise us at all, Geller suggests, "Wisdom was a determinedly international and humanistic tradition. The wise of all nations communicated with each other; genres, themes, and even language crossed boundaries freely."[7] While the Deuteronomistic school turned inward to focus on Israel's uniqueness, the Wisdom school faced outward to make connections between Hebrew philosophy and the other great intellectual traditions in the known world.

Wisdom literature often supports a universalist theology: If we look carefully, we can see a definite strand of universalism in the theology of the Old Testament. Not everybody believed that the Israelites were uniquely favored by God. Take the story of Jonah, often seen as heavily influenced by the Wisdom tradition. God instructs Jonah to go to Nineveh, the capital of the Assyrian Empire, and call its people to repent. After the famous misadventure with the great fish, Jonah goes to Nineveh and, with virtually no effort, so thoroughly converts the people that even the animals repent in sackcloth and ashes (Jonah 3:7–8). This is a wonderful story of God's love for all people—Chosen or otherwise. As we saw in Chapter Eight, Job, too, has a strong universalist message: God can and does interact with people of all races and cultures. Yahweh is not just the God of Israel; He is the God of everybody.

The prominence of the Wisdom tradition in the final version of the Hebrew Bible—a tradition that often conflicts directly with the other

---

7. Geller, "The Religion of the Bible," 2038.

strands of thought that went into its composition—shows us very clearly that the Old Testament is much richer and more complex than many of us realize. It is not just a library of different texts; it is a library of different opinions, different perspectives, and different values that often conflict sharply with each other. But this is just another way of saying that the Hebrew Bible is the record of a vibrant, dynamic, pluralistic culture and not the story of a bunch of sheep.

The Wisdom of Solomon: Proverbs and Ecclesiastes

The most important heroes of the Deuteronomistic and Priestly narratives are, respectively, the prophet Moses and the High Priest Aaron. The most important hero of the Wisdom tradition is Solomon the Wise—the mighty king, temple builder, baby splitter, and the greatest sage in Israel's history. The Wisdom writers credited Solomon with two of the three pure Wisdom books in the Bible—Proverbs and Ecclesiastes—as well as with the Song of Solomon and with the deuterocanonical Book of Wisdom. Like most attributions in the Old Testament, these should be considered honorary dedications and not statements of authorship. The Hebrews did not understand authorship the way we do today. Nearly every book in the Hebrew canon was produced and refined over many generations, with different authors and editors contributing to the final form. None of them ever signed their name, and nobody expected them to.

But they did often link their works with great figures of the past: Moses and the Pentateuch, David and the Psalms, and Solomon and the four books attributed to him. We know from textual and linguistic evidence that these books had a much later composition date than such attributions would permit. But we can learn a lot about the various schools of thought by their attributions. For example, the fact that both the Book of Proverbs and the Book of Ecclesiastes are attributed to Solomon shows that the Solomonic tradition influenced nearly every aspect of Wisdom literature, as these two books present starkly different philosophies of both divine and human nature.

The Book of Proverbs, along with the handful of Psalms considered "Wisdom Psalms"[8] and the twenty-eighth chapter of Job, are the chief biblical examples of the pious and positive strand of Wisdom literature that Crenshaw categorizes as "family wisdom."[9] This sort of wisdom distills

---

8. See Chapter 7, note 7, for a list of generally accepted "Wisdom Psalms."
9. Crenshaw, *Old Testament Wisdom*, 79.

cultural experience into short aphorisms like "actions speak louder than words" or "you can lead a horse to water, but you can't make him drink." Crenshaw refers to this as family wisdom because it is almost always taught in the home. Parents use these proverbs to teach their children how to prosper financially ("strike while the iron is hot"), form good relationships ("beauty is only skin deep"), and avoid danger ("look before you leap").

The biblical Book of Proverbs is really an anthology made up of a number of different source texts. It contains several long poems (2 and 7) and a fascinating comparison between the Lady Wisdom and the Harlot of Folly (8 and 9). But the core of the book, comprising chapters 10 through 23, consists of the two-line Wisdom sayings associated with King Solomon. The advice in this section is eminently practical. A few examples:

> Where there is much talking, there is no lack of transgressing,
> But he who curbs his tongue shows sense. (10:19)

> When arrogance appears, disgrace follows,
> But wisdom is with those who are unassuming. (11:2)

> He who loves discipline loves knowledge;
> He who spurns reproof is a brutish man. (12:1)

> A simple person believes anything;
> A clever man ponders his course. (14:15)

> A gentle response allays wrath;
> A harsh word provokes anger. (15:1)

> He who seeks love overlooks faults,
> But he who harps on a matter alienates his friend. (17:9)

> Even a fool, if he keeps silent, is deemed wise;
> Intelligent, if he seals his lips. (17:28)

> To answer a man before hearing him out
> Is foolish and disgraceful. (18:13)

Much of this advice stands the test of time remarkably well. It is still a bad idea to alienate a friend by harping on a matter, soft answers still turn away wrath, hearing people out is still an important skill to learn, and curbing one's tongue remains the best thing to do in many situations. The modern self-help industry has done very little to improve on the wisdom of the Hebrew sages.

One of the most famous verses in Proverbs reads, "The beginning of wisdom is fear of the Lord" (9:10). This is significant, as "the fear of the Lord" is the closest that Ancient Hebrew can come to our word "religion."

The authors of the Proverbs follow through with this in almost every chapter. "Blessings light upon the head of the righteous / But lawlessness covers the mouth of the wicked" (10:6), reads one verse from the aphoristic core. And another: "A good man earns the favor of the LORD, / A man of intrigues, His condemnation" (12:2). Throughout Proverbs, the major contrasts—wisdom/folly, righteousness/wickedness, and happiness/misery—are weaved into a single opposition: wise people are righteous and therefore they prosper, fools are wicked and therefore they suffer.

The Book of Ecclesiastes begs to differ. Ecclesiastes presents itself as the work of the great sage "Koheleth," son of David and king of Jerusalem and Israel—a description that can only apply to Solomon. Unlike the versified Proverbs, nearly all of Ecclesiastes is in prose. But this is a minor difference. The major difference between the two books lies in their radically different outlooks on life. The main theme of Proverbs is that following God makes people happy because God alone has access to true wisdom. The main theme of Ecclesiastes, on the other hand, is that nothing much matters because we are all going to die.

The author of Ecclesiastes is haunted by the idea that death cancels out every distinction that we make among ourselves—including the distinction between wisdom and foolishness:

> My thoughts also turned to appraising wisdom and madness and folly. I found that
>
> > Wisdom is superior to folly
> > As light is superior to darkness;
> > A wise man has his eyes in his head,
> > Whereas a fool walks in darkness.
>
> But I also realized that the same fate awaits them both. So I reflected: "The fate of the fool is also destined for me; to what advantage, then, have I been wise?" And I came to the conclusion that that too was futile, because the wise man, just like the fool, is not remembered forever; for, as the succeeding days roll by, both are forgotten. Alas, the wise man dies, just like the fool!
>
> And so I loathed life. For I was distressed by all that goes on under the sun, because everything is futile and pursuit of wind. (2:12–17)

From the beginning, Koheleth posits the random and unpredictable world that God forces Job to acknowledge in the finale. "Sometimes a good man perishes in spite of his goodness, and sometimes a wicked one endures in spite of his wickedness," he insists, "so don't overdo goodness and don't act the wise man to excess, or you may be dumfounded" (7:15–16). And there is no relying on wisdom, which is not sufficient to the task (7:29; 10:1) or on God, who is completely inscrutable (7:13–14).

So how should we live? According to Koheleth, we should seek out whatever pleasures we can wrest from life and consider them sufficient:

> Thus I realized that the only worthwhile thing there is for them is to enjoy themselves and do what is good in their lifetime; also, that whenever a man does eat and drink and get enjoyment out of all his wealth, it is a gift of God. (3:12–13)

> I saw that there is nothing better for man than to enjoy his possessions, since that is his portion. For who can enable him to see what will happen afterward? (3:22)

> Only this, I have found, is a real good: that one should eat and drink and get pleasure with all the gains he makes under the sun, during the numbered days of life that God has given him; for that is his portion. (5:17)

> Enjoy happiness with a woman you love all the fleeting days of life that have been granted to you under the sun—all your fleeting days. For that alone is what you can get out of life and out of the means you acquire under the sun. Whatever it is in your power to do, do with all your might. For there is no action, no reasoning, no learning, no wisdom in Sheol, where you are going. (9:9–10)

These are the sorts of "eat, drink, and be merry" passages that we might expect to find in the writings of Epicurus or Horace. They have little to do with the pious moralizing of Proverbs. And yet both Proverbs and Ecclesiastes fit squarely within the Hebrew Wisdom tradition. This is true because wisdom is not so much a compilation of answers as it is a set of questions—all some variant of the great question, "How does one live well in the world that exists?" Because the writers of Proverbs and Ecclesiastes saw the existing world differently, they came up with different answers. But both books focus on the world that exists now; neither says anything at all about ritual purity or about Israel's covenant with God. These things were of no concern to the writers of Wisdom literature, who were instead trying to discover the best ways to be human beings.

Job in the Wisdom Tradition

One way to describe Job might be as the story of a man who thinks he is living in the world of Proverbs but finds himself trapped in that of Ecclesiastes with no way to escape. He desperately wants to live in a world where righteousness prospers and wickedness does not—and where the fear of the Lord really is the beginning of wisdom. But his life just does not work out that way. As they collide with each other in Job, the radically different worldviews of Proverbs and Ecclesiastes begin to make sense as elements of the same tradition. Though the Job poet acknowledges the reality of Koheleth's worldview, he sees it as a tragedy to be mourned, and perhaps a problem to be solved—but not as an invitation to eat, drink, and try to find things to be merry about.

Job insists that the moral framework of Proverbs, in which goodness matters and wisdom leads to happiness, is worth believing in. And even if we cannot believe in it, we can certainly aspire to it. This is where Job departs so sharply from Ecclesiastes. Rather than follow Koheleth down the rabbit hole of moral resignation, Job dares to disturb the universe. We can discern the spark of continued defiance deep inside of his narrative. If God is not willing to create a just world, then maybe we can do it ourselves. Maybe we are the only ones who ever could. Maybe this is what God has been saying all along.

At their core, however, Proverbs, Ecclesiastes, and Job all teach us how to live. As we peel back Job's layers, we find solid advice about things that matter in our day-to-day lives. Though the main purpose of the poem is not to reduce practical wisdom to neat aphorisms, I suspect that a collection of "Job-inspired proverbs" would be as useful as anything in the Bible for living more comfortably in the world—even a world 2,500 years removed from the world of the poet. Such aphorisms might include:

From Satan's Perspective

- Do not get in arguments with people about things they know a lot more about than you do; you will lose and look foolish at the same time. This is especially true if they are omniscient or all-powerful.
- If you lose a bet, stop. If you keep going, you will just lose more. Quit while you are only moderately behind.

From Job's Perspective

- Just because you do not understand the reason for something does not mean that there is no reason for it; it just means that your understanding is limited.
- Do not become easily offended when people give well-meaning advice, even if it is completely inappropriate. Remember that they are doing their best to love you, even if they are not always very good at it.

- Just because you are unhappy does not mean that the universe is flawed. It is not the universe's job to make you happy.
- You have biases and fragilities that determine how you see the world. Understand the limitations of your perspective and show humility in the presence of other points of view.
- You cannot control everything that happens to you, but you can always control how you respond.
- Do not look to other people for comfort; ultimately, you have to learn how to do it yourself.
- It is okay with God if you complain about stuff; omniscient beings can handle petitions.
- Do not scrape—it just makes things worse.

From the Comforter's Perspective

- If you do not understand what somebody is going through, do not try to explain it. Just listen to them and love them.
- You do not have to worry about protecting God. God can protect Himself. Your responsibility is to protect the people who cannot protect themselves.
- Every effect has a cause, but not every effect has a cause that you are capable of understanding.
- Sometimes being a good friend means doing things that will make you religiously or ideologically uncomfortable. Be a good friend anyway.
- Sometimes people bring their own suffering on themselves, and sometimes they do not. You do not have to decide; you just have to love them.
- You do not have the foggiest idea what God is thinking—so stop pretending.
- Nobody likes a suck-up, not even God.

And that is just for starters. By teaching us how to be better friends and happier people the Book of Job earns its place in the Wisdom tradition. But it really is not fair to reduce a great poem to aphorisms. This takes out all the poetry, and a lot of the meaning, because the shape and texture of poems mean things too. And this is especially true in Job. The form of the book works against any decisive paraphrase of its meaning. By combining a prose frame and a poetic dialogue, Job invites us to see the story of its hero from two distinct perspectives. By building most of the poem around dialogues between Job and his interlocutors, the poet dares us to derive stable meaning from multiple flawed points of view.

When we read Job, or any great work of literature, we must combine our own perspective with that of another powerful mind. This is why great literature stays great—it gives every new generation of readers the opportunity to apply its insights to a whole new set of issues and problems. The Job poet did not imagine the Holocaust as such, but he understood human nature—and that allowed him to construct a poem that could be relevant to the post-Holocaust world in ways that inferior poets could never manage. This is one of the things that great literature can do.

Another thing that great literature can do is help us discover what we already know—or so the Wisdom writers believed. Wisdom literature grounds its truth in recognition, rather than inductive or deductive reasoning. It does not prove things true; it simply asserts them and relies on us to recognize truths that we have always sort of known but never really thought about. The Book of Proverbs likens this to drawing water from a deep well:

> Sagacity in a man's mind is like deep water;
> The intelligent person will draw from it.(20:5)[10]

This image of deep water is particularly powerful: it suggests something that is already there, but it is buried and inaccessible without an equally deep well. So too, the Wisdom books suggest, are the reservoirs of wisdom in the human mind. This wisdom does not need to be placed there by an external authority; rather, it needs to be made accessible, unhidden, and revealed to the mind that has always contained it. This is how great literature produces its greatest insights. It works about the same way as what Latter-day Saints call "personal revelation."

The Book of Job is a difficult text. Its multiple voices each present us with a piece of the truth. But they never quite go together into a single, unified message. Astute readers will have already noticed that my own interpretations of Job in this book are not all compatible with each other. In some places, I have assumed a radical disjuncture between the frame and the poem, but in others, I treat them as part of the same narrative flow. Sometimes, I am on Job's side and sometimes I am on God's side—and, in a few places, I have good things to say about both the Comforters and the Devil. Even if I wanted to be completely consistent about these things, I could not, for Job is a poem about (among so many other things) the impossibility of finding the truth in a single perspective.

---

10. I use the translation by R.B.Y. Scott, *The Anchor Bible: Proverbs and Ecclesiastes*, 119.

This is why I believe that imaginative literature is completely compatible with divine revelation. If we know how to read it, a great poem can teach us things that nothing else can teach us in ways that will stay with us forever. For centuries, well-meaning people have buried some of the most important insights in the scriptures by trying to subsume all truth into a category called "historical fact." I will continue to insist that there is absolutely no reason for us to do this. Calling something a "poem" or a "story" does not diminish it, nor does saying that something did not happen imply that it is not true. The Book of Job is a magnificent work of literature that teaches us important truths about suffering, friendship, human nature, and God. And it teaches us these things by being a poem.

The Wisdom writing of the Bible, including the Book of Job, is built on the premise that literature can produce great insights and serve as a vehicle for revelation. A great poem can clarify something that we suddenly realize we have always known. A powerful story will give us a framework for thinking about something we have always considered important but never been able to describe. A well-wrought aphorism will show us something about ourselves that we have never considered before. This is what "being true" means in the Wisdom tradition.

To read Job as a work of Wisdom literature, then, does not require that we dismiss it, or relegate it to a lesser status than "history." Documentary history as we understand it today is only a few hundred years old. Imaginative literature, on the other hand, is a human universal. Examples of parables— some heroic and some cautionary—can be found throughout human culture. And what we call the Old Testament is actually a library that contains an entire people's history, law, prophecy, and literature. It would be remarkable if such a collection did not contain some texts designed to be read primarily as literature, just as it would be tragic if the collective consciousness of a great people contained no great poetry.

Bibliography

Adorno, Theodor W. *Negative Dialectics*. Translated by E. B. Ashton. New York: Seabury Press, 1973.

Alexander, Thomas. *Mormonism in Transition: A History of the Latter-day Saints, 1890–1930*. Salt Lake City: Greg Kofford Books, 2012.

Alter, Robert. *The Art of Biblical Poetry*. New York: Basic Books, 1986.

_____. *The Wisdom Books: Job, Proverbs, and Ecclesiastes: A Translation with Commentary*. New York: Norton, 2010.

Austin, Michael. *New Testaments: Cognition, Closure, and the Figural Logic of the Sequel*. University of Delaware Press, 2012.

_____. *Useful Fictions: Evolution, Anxiety, and the Origins of Literature*. University of Nebraska Press, 2010.

Bokovoy, David. *Authoring the Old Testament: Genesis–Deuteronomy*. Salt Lake City: Greg Kofford Books, 2014.

Brown, Hugh B. "God Is the Gardner." BYU Commencement Address, 1968. Archived at https://www.youtube.com/watch?v=oDrhvm9EnJ4.

Childs, Brevard S. *Introduction to the Old Testament as Scripture*. Philadelphia: Fortress Press, 1976.

Crenshaw, James L. *Old Testament Wisdom: An Introduction*. Louisville, Ky.: Westminster John Knox Press, 1998.

Frankel, Victor. *Man's Search for Meaning*. 3rd ed. New York: Touchstone, 1984.

Frost, Robert. "A Masque of Reason." In *The Voice out of the Whirlwind: The Book of Job* by Ralph E. Hone. San Francisco: Chandler, 1972.

Frye, Northrup. *The Great Code*. New York: Harcourt Brace Jovanovich, 1982.

Gammie, John G. and Leo G. Purdue, eds. *The Sage in Israel and the Ancient Near East*. Winona Lake, Ind.: Eisenbrauns, 1990.

Geller, Stephen A. "The Religion of the Bible." In *The Jewish Study Bible*, edited by Adele Berlin and Marc Zvi Brettler. Oxford University Press: 2004.

Glatzer, Nahum N., ed. *The Dimensions of Job*. New York: Schocken, 1969.

Gordis, Robert. "Elihu the Intruder." In *Biblical and Other Studies*, edited by Alexander Altmann. Harvard University Press, 1963.

Grant, Michael. *The History of Ancient Israel*. New York: Scribner's, 1984.

Gregory the Great. *Morals on the Book of Job.* Translated by Members of the English Church. 4 vols. Oxford: John Henry Parker, 1844.

Hardin, Sylvia K. *Job's Belief and Faithfulness Rewarded by God.* Bloomington, Ind.: Xlibris, 2013.

Jung, C.G. *God's Answer to Job.* Princeton University Press, 1958.

Kafka, Franz. *The Trial.* Translated by Willa and Edwin Muir. New York: Schocken Books, 1968.

Kant, Immanuel. "On the Miscarriage of All Philosophical Trials in Theodicy." In *Religion and Rational Theology*, edited and translated by Allen W. Wood and George Di Giovanni. Cambridge University Press, 2001.

Keats, John. *The Complete Poems.* Edited by John Barnard. New York: Penguin, 1977.

Kolitz, Zvi. *Yosl Rakover Talks to God.* New York: Vintage, 2000.

Kraeling, Emil G. "A Theodicy—and More." In *The Dimensions of Job*, by Nahum N. Glatzer. New York: Schocken, 1969.

Kushner, Harold S. *When Bad Things Happen to Good People.* New York: Schocken, 1978.

_____. *The Book of Job: When Bad Things Happened to a Good Person.* New York: Schocken, 2012.

Larrimore, Mark. *The Book of Job: A Biography.* Princeton University Press, 2013.

Linafelt, Tod, ed. *Strange Fire: Reading the Bible after the Holocaust.* New York University Press, 2000.

MacLeish, Archibald. "God Has Need of Man." In *The Dimensions of Job*, edited by Nahum N. Glatzer, 278–86. New York: Schocken, 1969.

_____. *J.B.* New York: Houghton Mifflin, 1956.

Maimonides, Moses. *The Guide for the Perplexed.* Translated by M. Frieländer. New York: Dover, 1956.

Murray, Gilbert. "Beyond Good and Evil." In *The Dimensions of Job*, edited by Nahum Glatzer. New York: Shocken Books, 1969.

Newsom, Carol A. *The Book of Job: A Contest of Moral Imaginations.* Oxford University Press, 2003.

Noth, Martin. *The Deuteronomistic History.* Translated by E.W. Nicholson. Sheffield, UK. In *Journal for the Study of the Old Testament.* Supplemental Series, 15, 1981.

Old Testament Student Manual 1 Kings–Malachi. 3rd ed. Church of Jesus Christ of Latter-day Saints, 2003.

Ozick, Cynthia. "The Impious Impatience of Job." In *The American Scholar* 67.4 (Autumn 1998), 15–25.

Pope, Alexander. *Poetry and Prose of Alexander Pope.* Edited by Aubrey Williams. Boston: Houghton Mifflin, 1969.

Pope, Marvin. *The Anchor Bible: Job.* New York: Anchor/Doubleday, 1965.

Russell, Jeffrey Burton. *The Devil: Perceptions of Evil from Antiquity to Primitive Christianity.* Cornell University Press, 1977.

Scott, R.B.Y. *The Anchor Bible: Proverbs and Ecclesiastes.* New York: Anchor/Doubleday, 1965.

Sill, Sterling W. *The Law of the Harvest*. Salt Lake City: Bookcraft, 1963.

Stillinger, Jack, ed. *Twentieth Century Interpretations of Keats's Odes: A Collection of Critical Essays*. Englewood Cliffs, N.J.: Prentice-Hall, 1968.

Tanner, John S. "Why Latter-Day Saints Should Read Job." *Sunstone* 14:4 (August 1990), 38–47.

Terrien, Samuel. *Job: The Poet of Existence*. Indianapolis: Bobbs-Merrill, 1957.

Voltaire. *Candide*. Translated by John Butt. New York: Penguin, 1947.

von Goethe, Johann Wolfgang. *Faust*. Translated by Walter Kaufman. New York: Random House, 1961.

Von Rad, Gerhard. *Wisdom in Israel*. Nashville, Tenn.: Abingdon Press, 1972.

Weil, Simone. *Gravity and Grace*. London: Ark, 1952.

Wells, H. G. *The Undying Fire*. Nashville, Tenn.: Broadman & Holman, 1998.

Whitman, Walt. *The Works of Walt Whitman*. Hertfordshire, UK: Wordsworth Poetry Library, 1995.

Wiesel, Elie. *Day*. Translated by Anne Borchardt. New York: Hill and Wang, 2006. Previously published as *The Accident*. New York: Hill and Wang, 1962.

_____. *Messengers of God*. Translated by Marion Wiesel. New York: Summit Books, 1976.

_____. *Night*. Translated by Marion Wiesel. New York: Hill & Wang, 2006.

_____. *The Trial of God*. Translated by Marion Wiesel. New York: Schocken, 1979.

Index

and the afterlife, 38, 40, 90
and the Bible, 103–17
Church of Jesus Christ of Latter-day
    Saints, x–xi, 10, 112–13
    and the Bible, 15
Cinderella, 4–5, 38, 41
Clockmaker God, 121–22
cognitive science, 26
Comforters. *See* Job, Comforters.
Conant, James B., 80
Cornelius, 112
Cowley, Abraham, xi, 2
Coyote, 30
Crenshaw, James L., 137–38, 140

D

Dante, 20
Darius the Great, 36
David, 107, 140, 142
Defoe, Daniel, xi
deism, 121–22
deus absconditus, 79, 80
Deuteronomistic history, 92–98, 100–101
Deuteronomistic Source (D), xiii, 68,
    93, 110, 136–37, 139, 140
Deuteronomy, Book of, 92, 93–94,
    100–101, 104, 112–13
Divine Comedy. See Dante.
Doctrine and Covenants, 15, 123
Don Quixote. See Cervantes, Miguel de.

E–F

Ecclesiastes, Book of, 17, 95, 137, 142–43
Egypt, 16, 67, 82, 108, 139
El Cid, 16
Elihu, xiii, 60, 64, 69–73, 116, 123, 129
Eliot, T.S., 25
Eliphaz, 12, 44, 45–52, 64, 97, 98, 114–16
Epic of Gilgamesh, 16, 27
epode, 62
Esther, Book of, 17, 126, 139
Euripides, 12, 25
Exodus, Book of, 6, 67, 108

Ezekiel, Book of, 92, 107
fairy tales, 5, 18–19
Family Home Evening, 110
Faulkner, William, 3
Faust. See Goethe, Johann Wolfgang von.
Frankel, Victor, 42
Freud, Sigmund, 80
Frost, Robert, x, 89
    A Masque of Reason, 89–90
Frye, Northrup, 75

G

gaʾal, 104–7, 117
Gammie, John G., 137
Geller, Stephen A., 136
genocide, 93–94
Glatzer, Nahum, 80
goʾel. See gaʾal.
Goethe, Johann Wolfgang von, ix, 16,
    29, 31–32, 33
Good Samaritan, Parable of, 16, 20,
    114–16
Gordis, Robert, 72
Grant, Heber J., 17
Grant, Michael, 92–93
Gregory the Great, 109
Gulliver's Travels. See Swift, Jonathan.

H–I

haiku, 5, 23
Hardin, Sylvia K., 92
Hegel, Georg Wilhelm Friedrich, ix
Heinlein, Robert A., x
Herod, 108
Herodotus, 36
Higher Criticism, 18
Hittites, 6
Holocaust, 42, 123–34, 146
Holy of Holies, 72
home teaching, 110
Homer, 5, 13
Hosea, Book of, 108
Hugo, Victor, ix, 13

Other titles in the
CONTEMPORARY STUDIES
IN SCRIPTURE series

Authoring the Old Testament: Genesis–Deuteronomy

David Bokovoy

Paperback, ISBN: 978-1-58958-588-1
Hardcover, ISBN: 978-1-58958-675-8

For the last two centuries, biblical scholars have made discoveries and insights about the Old Testament that have greatly changed the way in which the authorship of these ancient scriptures has been understood. In the first of three volumes spanning the entire Hebrew Bible, David Bokovoy dives into the Pentateuch, showing how and why textual criticism has led biblical scholars today to understand the first five books of the Bible as an amalgamation of multiple texts into a single, though often complicated narrative; and he discusses what implications those have for Latter-day Saint understandings of the Bible and modern scripture.

Praise for *Authoring the Old Testament*:

"*Authoring the Old Testament* is a welcome introduction, from a faithful Latter-day Saint perspective, to the academic world of Higher Criticism of the Hebrew Bible. . . . [R]eaders will be positively served and firmly impressed by the many strengths of this book, coupled with Bokovoy's genuine dedication to learning by study and also by faith." — John W. Welch, editor, *BYU Studies Quarterly*

"Bokovoy provides a lucid, insightful lens through which disciple-students can study intelligently LDS scripture. This is first rate scholarship made accessible to a broad audience—nourishing to the heart and mind alike." — Fiona Givens, co-author, *The God Who Weeps: How Mormonism Makes Sense of Life*

"I repeat: this is one of the most important books on Mormon scripture to be published recently. . . . [*Authoring the Old Testament*] has the potential to radically expand understanding and appreciation for not only the Old Testament, but scripture in general. It's really that good. Read it. Share it with your friends. Discuss it." — David Tayman, The Improvement Era: A Mormon Blog

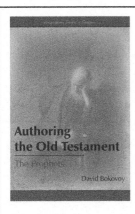

Authoring the Old Testament:
The Prophets

David Bokovoy

Paperback, ISBN: 978-1-58958-663-5
Hardcover, ISBN: 978-1-58958-676-5

For the last two centuries, biblical scholars have made discoveries and insights about the Old Testament that have greatly changed the way in which the authorship of these ancient scriptures have been understood. In the second of three volumes spanning the entire Hebrew Bible, David Bokovoy dives into the histories and prophets, showing what textual criticism has led biblical scholars today to understand of these books of the Bible, and what implications those have for Latter-day Saint understandings of the Bible and modern scripture.

Praise for *Authoring the Old Testament*:

"David Bokovoy is a solid scholar of the Hebrew Bible whose goal is to help Latter-day Saints as they step out of the ark into the broad daylight of serious scriptural engagement. His new book *Authoring the Old Testament: Genesis—Deuteronomy* is the first part of a much-needed introduction for Mormons to the academic world of historical criticism. . . . Members of the Church will be introduced to some of the results of over a century of biblical scholarship they've likely never heard about as they emerge from the protective ark to enjoy discussing things in the sunshine." — Neal A. Maxwell Institute for Religious Scholarship

"*Authoring the Old Testament* opens up a much-needed dialog on the historical-critical approach for Latter-day Saints. It demonstrates, in insightful and meaningful ways, how the historical-critical method can be faithfully applied to the Book of Mormon, the Book of Moses, and the Book of Abraham. In my view, this book is a must for those seeking to incorporate the best of biblical scholarship in their personal or professional scripture study." — Brian Hauglid, author, A Textual History of the Book of Abraham: Manuscripts and Editions

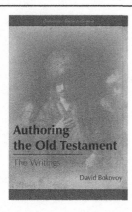

Authoring the Old Testament:
The Writings

David Bokovoy

Paperback, ISBN: 978-1-58958-664-2
Hardcover, ISBN: 978-1-58958-677-2

For the last two centuries, biblical scholars have made discoveries and insights about the Old Testament that have greatly changed the way in which the authorship of these ancient scriptures have been understood. In the last of three volumes spanning the entire Hebrew Bible, David Bokovoy dives into the writings of the prophets, showing what textual criticism has led biblical scholars today to understand of these books of the Bible, and what implications those have for Latter-day Saint understandings of the Bible and modern scripture.

Praise for *Authoring the Old Testament*:

"Bringing fresh insights to the Old Testament, a book like this for a Latter-day Saint audience is long overdue. Bokovoy skillfully weaves together biblical scholars with LDS leaders and texts to demonstrate the religious benefits of confronting post-Enlightenment readings of the Bible, clarifying long-standing questions. Charting a middle path between conservative inerrancy and secular dismissal of biblical texts, this book refreshingly expounds on the nature of ancient and modern scripture." — Taylor G. Petrey, Lucinda Hinsdale Stone Assistant Professor of Religion, Kalamazoo College

"Bokovoy's *Authoring the Old Testament: Genesis—Deuteronomy* provides an important resource in making many of the intricacies of higher criticism available to Latter-day Saint readers in an accessible fashion. Because Bokovoy has geared it to an LDS audience, he has also been able to make interesting suggestions for critically reading Restoration texts. Regardless of one's final position on the Documentary Hypothesis, this book should be basic reading for serious LDS students of the Bible." — Eric D. Huntsman, Coordinator of Ancient Near Eastern Studies, Brigham Young University

Re-reading Job: Understanding the Ancient World's Greatest Poem

Michael Austin

Paperback, ISBN: 978-1-58958-667-3
Hardcover, ISBN: 978-1-58958-668-0

Job is perhaps the most difficult to understand of all books in the Bible. While a cursory reading of the text seems to relay a simple story of a righteous man whose love for God was tested through life's most difficult of challenges and rewarded for his faith through those trials, a closer reading of Job presents something far more complex and challenging. The majority of the text is a work of poetry that authors and artists through the centuries have recognized as being one of--if not the--greatest poem of the ancient world.

In *Re-reading Job: Understanding the Ancient World's Greatest Poem*, author Michael Austin shows how most readers have largely misunderstood this important work of scripture and provides insights that enable us to re-read Job in a drastically new way. In doing so, he shows that the story of Job is far more than that simple story of faith, trials, and blessings that we have all come to know, but is instead a subversive and complex work of scripture meant to inspire readers to rethink all that they thought they knew about God.

Praise for *Re-reading Job*:

"In this remarkable book, Michael Austin employs his considerable skills as a commentator to shed light on the most challenging text in the entire Hebrew Bible. Without question, readers will gain a deeper appreciation for this extraordinary ancient work through Austin's learned analysis. Rereading Job signifies that Latter-day Saints are entering a new age of mature biblical scholarship. It is an exciting time, and a thrilling work." — David Bokovoy, author, *Authoring the Old Testament*

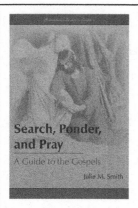

Search, Ponder, and Pray:
A Guide to the Gospels

Julie M. Smith

Paperback, ISBN: 978-1-58958-671-0
Hardcover, ISBN: 978-1-58958-672-7

From the author's preface:

During my graduate studies in theology, I came to realize that there is quite a bit of work done in the field of biblical studies that can be useful to members of the Church as they read the scriptures. Unfortunately, academic jargon usually makes these works impenetrable, and I was unable to find many publications that made this research accessible to the non-specialist. In this book, I have endeavored to present some of the most interesting insights of biblical scholars—in plain language.

It was also important to me that I not present the work of these scholars in a way that would make you feel obligated to accept their conclusions. Since scholars rarely agree with each other, I can see no reason why you should feel compelled to agree with them. My hope is that the format of this book will encourage you to view the insights of scholars as the beginning of a discussion instead of the end of an argument. In some cases, I have presented the positions of scholars (and even some critics of the Church) specifically to encourage you to develop your own responses to these arguments based on your personal scripture study. I certainly don't agree with every idea in this book.

I encourage you to read the Introduction. Although I have endeavored to keep it as short as possible, there are several issues related to the interpretation of the scriptures that should be addressed before you begin interpreting.

It is my experience that thoughtful scripture study leads to personal revelation. I hope that through the process of searching the scriptures, pondering these questions, and praying about the answers, you will be edified.

Life is full of unanswered questions. Here are over 4,500 more of them.

Beholding the Tree of Life:
A Rabbinic Approach to
the Book of Mormon

Bradley J. Kramer

Paperback, ISBN: 978-1-58958-701-4
Hardcover, ISBN: 978-1-58958-702-1

Too often readers approach the Book of Mormon simply as a collection of quotations, an inspired anthology to be scanned quickly and routinely recited. In Beholding the Tree of Life Bradley J. Kramer encourages his readers to slow down, to step back, and to contemplate the literary qualities of the Book of Mormon using interpretive techniques developed by Talmudic and post-Talmudic rabbis. Specifically, Kramer shows how to read the Book of Mormon closely, in levels, paying attention to the details of its expression as well as to its overall connection to the Hebrew Scriptures—all in order to better appreciate the beauty of the Book of Mormon and its limitless capacity to convey divine meaning.

Praise for *Authoring the Old Testament*:

"Latter-day Saints have claimed the Book of Mormon as the keystone of their religion, but it presents itself first and foremost as a Jewish narrative. *Beholding the Tree of Life* is the first book I have seen that attempts to situate the Book of Mormon by paying serious attention to its Jewish literary precedents and ways of reading scripture. It breaks fresh ground in numerous ways that enrich an LDS understanding of the scriptures and that builds bridges to a potential Jewish readership." — Terryl L. Givens, author of *By the Hand of Mormon: The American Scripture that Launched a New World Religion*

"Bradley Kramer has done what someone ought to have done long ago, used the methods of Jewish scripture interpretation to look closely at the Book of Mormon. Kramer has taken the time and put in the effort required to learn those methods from Jewish teachers. He explains what he has learned clearly and carefully. And then he shows us the fruit of that learning by applying it to the Book of Mormon. The results are not only interesting, they are inspiring. This is one of those books that, on reading it, I thought 'I wish I'd written that!'" — James E. Faulconer, author of *The Book of Mormon Made Harder* and *Faith, Philosophy, Scripture*

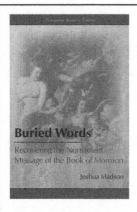

Buried Words:
Recovering the Nonviolent Message
of the Book of Mormon

Joshua Madson

Paperback, ISBN: 978-1-58958-673-4
Hardcover, ISBN: 978-1-58958-674-1

At face value the Book of Mormon offers complex and often competing perspectives on war and violence. On one hand you have the Anti-Nephi-Lehites who buried their weapons and covenanted to never again engage in violence; on the other you have the Nephite captain, Moroni, who actively proclaims a form of just war theory and is praised by the warrior-prophet Mormon. While the former is often admired but looked-over as an idealized but impractical approach, it is the latter—the heroic Captain Moroni—who is repeatedly made the exemplar of righteous militarism in the Latter-day Saint tradition.

In *Buried Words: Recovering the Nonviolent Message of the Book of Mormon*, Joshua Madson argues that the record of the Nephites should not be read as a collection of proof-text-ready passages and isolated moral narratives, but that it should instead be read as an entire epic narrative that acts as a warning to those who would put their trust in violence. Madson shows how the Nephites' own self-understanding is one built on a foundation of bloodshed—a self-understanding that continually perpetuates itself until it results in their ultimate demise. Rather than a justification for participating in violence, Madson argues that, as a whole, the Book of Mormon acts as a voice and warning against warfare and pleads for all its readers to seek peace without bloodshed.

According to Their Language: The King James Bible in the Book of Mormon

Colby Townsend

Paperback, ISBN: 978-1-58958-669-7
Hardcover, ISBN: 978-1-58958-670-3

Since its publication readers of the Book of Mormon have recognized the linguistic presence of the King James Bible in the Book of Mormon. While the selections from Isaiah, the Sermon on the Mount, and other lengthy passages are easily noticed, the vast suffusion of the KJV language in the Book of Mormon is less obvious to most readers.

In this painstakingly detailed examination, Colby Townsend provides an annotated study of the direct and indirect ways in which the language of the King James Bible pervades nearly every verse of the Book of Mormon. This monumental work will prove to be an invaluable resource in understanding the sacred text.

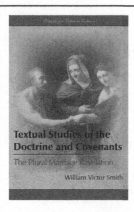

Textual Studies of
the Doctrine and Covenants:
The Plural Marriage Revelation

William Victor Smith

Paperback, ISBN: 978-1-58958-690-1
Hardcover, ISBN: 978-1-58958-691-8

The July 12, 1843 revelation was the last of Joseph Smith's formal written revelations, and it was a watershed in Mormonism for many reasons. *Textual Studies of the Doctrine and Covenants: The Plural Marriage Revelation* constitutes a study of the text of that revelation, its genetic profile as an endpoint for a number of trajectories in Mormon thought, liturgy, and priestly cosmology, and a brief exploration of its historical impact and interpretation.

Also available from
GREG KOFFORD BOOKS

The Gift and Power: Translating the Book of Mormon

Brant A. Gardner

Hardcover, ISBN: 978-1-58958-131-9

From Brant A. Gardner, the author of the highly praised *Second Witness* commentaries on the Book of Mormon, comes *The Gift and Power: Translating the Book of Mormon*. In this first book-length treatment of the translation process, Gardner closely examines the accounts surrounding Joseph Smith's translation of the Book of Mormon to answer a wide spectrum of questions about the process, including: Did the Prophet use seerstones common to folk magicians of his time? How did he use them? And, what is the relationship to the golden plates and the printed text?

Approaching the topic in three sections, part 1 examines the stories told about Joseph, folk magic, and the translation. Part 2 examines the available evidence to determine how closely the English text replicates the original plate text. And part 3 seeks to explain how seer stones worked, why they no longer work, and how Joseph Smith could have produced a translation with them.

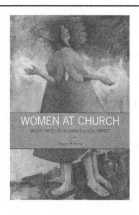

Women at Church: Magnifying LDS Women's Local Impact

Neylan McBaine

Paperback, ISBN: 978-1-58958-688-8

Women at Church is a practical and faithful guide to improving the way men and women work together at church. Looking at current administrative and cultural practices, the author explains why some women struggle with the gendered divisions of labor. She then examines ample real-life examples that are currently happening in local settings around the country that expand and reimagine gendered practices. Readers will understand how to evaluate possible pain points in current practices and propose solutions that continue to uphold all mandated church policies. Readers will be equipped with the tools they need to have respectful, empathetic and productive conversations about gendered practices in Church administration and culture.

Praise for *Women at Church*:

"Such a timely, faithful, and practical book! I suggest ordering this book in bulk to give to your bishopric, stake presidency, and all your local leadership to start a conversation on changing Church culture for women by letting our doctrine suggest creative local adaptations—Neylan McBaine shows the way!" — Valerie Hudson Cassler, author of *Women in Eternity, Women of Zion*

"A pivotal work replete with wisdom and insight. Neylan McBaine deftly outlines a workable programme for facilitating movement in the direction of the 'privileges and powers' promised the nascent Female Relief Society of Nauvoo." — Fiona Givens, co-author of *The God Who Weeps: How Mormonism Makes Sense of Life*

"In her timely and brilliant findings, Neylan McBaine issues a gracious invitation to rethink our assumptions about women's public Church service. Well researched, authentic, and respectful of the current Church administrative structure, McBaine shares exciting and practical ideas that address diverse needs and involve all members in the meaningful work of the Church." — Camille Fronk Olson, author of *Women of the Old Testament* and *Women of the New Testament*

Dead Wood and Rushing Water: Essays on Mormon Faith, Culture, and Family

Boyd Jay Petersen

Paperback, ISBN: 978-1-58958-658-1

For over a decade, Boyd Petersen has been an active voice in Mormon studies and thought. In essays that steer a course between apologetics and criticism, striving for the balance of what Eugene England once called the "radical middle," he explores various aspects of Mormon life and culture—from the Dream Mine near Salem, Utah, to the challenges that Latter-day Saints of the millennial generation face today.

Praise for _Dead Wood and Rushing Water_:

"_Dead Wood and Rushing Water_ gives us a reflective, striving, wise soul ruminating on his world. In the tradition of Eugene England, Petersen examines everything in his Mormon life from the gold plates to missions to dream mines to doubt and on to Glenn Beck, Hugh Nibley, and gender. It is a book I had trouble putting down." — Richard L. Bushman, author of _Joseph Smith: Rough Stone Rolling_

"Boyd Petersen is correct when he says that Mormons have a deep hunger for personal stories—at least when they are as thoughtful and well-crafted as the ones he shares in this collection." — Jana Riess, author of _The Twible_ and _Flunking Sainthood_

"Boyd Petersen invites us all to ponder anew the verities we hold, sharing in his humility, tentativeness, and cheerful confidence that our paths will converge in the end." — Terryl. L. Givens, author of _People of Paradox: A History of Mormon Culture_

Made in the USA
Monee, IL
24 November 2023

47176267R10114